Blind Sight

Blind Sight

ADELINE MOORE

About the Cover

The Aloe Plant soothes and calms. It is a bona fide wound healer, giving easily of itself, growing new leaves continuously—as long as it is properly nourished with just the right amount of sunlight, water, nutrients and time. However, with too much plucking, the plant cannot restore itself quickly enough to survive.

Like the aloe plant, we cannot have too much taken from us. We cannot neglect our need for nourishment and sustenance without realizing we will be depleted, desperate, and diseased.
To survive and thrive, we must live in awareness and balance.

Typeface used for front cover is Montserrat. Back cover text is set in Avenir.

© 2017 Adeline Moore
All rights reserved.
ISBN: 197790890X
ISBN 13: 9781977908902

This book is dedicated to the emotionally starved—the deprived who can become depraved simply because they did not receive affirmation of who they were and therefore could not become who they were meant to be.

Surrender yourself to the realization that you must get what you need to survive. Don't look in other places to find out what happened. That can come after the fact.

You must claw your way out of wherever you are. You must run into yourself on the bare, creaky floor of self-discovery. You must pray for the keenest insight that is humanly possible.

You must pray for a miracle.

One

BATTLE CRIES

This is the summer my mother died. It is just eight weeks after the funeral, and this vacation at the beach is the beginning of what it feels like to be free.

I think about my mother and some of the memories we made together. Sure, there was a lot to celebrate. She adored her grandchildren and made it to their birthday celebrations, high school and college graduations, weddings, and bridal and baby showers. She was proud when they began their professional careers and was interested in everything they did. She loved her grandchildren unconditionally.

But it was a different story with her five children. We were raised in a competitive environment in which we were compared to one another. One of us was more easygoing than the others. One of us was smarter or more generous. Another was too serious. Someone else was friendlier. No matter what we did—good or bad—we were continually reminded of our flaws. We were emotionally assaulted on all fronts, with nowhere to run and nowhere to hide.

- "Why can't you be more like your sister?"
- "Your brother is the only one who never answered me back."
- "You're disrespectful."
- "Our relationship has been up and down; you're not loyal."
- "You're too sensitive."
- "You're too serious."
- "Lighten up."
- "Let it go."
- "You care only about the kids."
- "You like to be the center of attention."
- "You think you know everything."
- "You're too bossy."

And then there were the more threatening, hurtful, insidiously controlling remarks.

- "I'm not going to tell you who said it, but I heard that someone doesn't like you very much."
- "I don't want to start trouble, but…"
- "I probably shouldn't tell you, but don't you want to know what _____ thinks about you?"
- "I would want to know if I were you."

Sadly, not only did she compare us to one another, but she also compared us to our extended family and friends and to anyone else who was doing better or who was more successful in his or her personal and professional life than we were. She made it part of her repertoire to tell us how "nice" other people were—how easygoing, good-natured, sweet, loyal, and *good to his or her mother* a person could be.

She made a point—in her inimitable way—of explaining in broad detail just how well someone else was doing, or how terrific someone else was—and hidden in this cryptic language was the crystal-clear message that we were not.

Now you might think there's nothing wrong with passing along good news. I agree. Under normal circumstances, there's not. But you'd have to know my mother—her agenda, her purpose, her intention, her tone, her expression, and her style in telling the story.

She was a master at using the strong points of a story to compare them with the weak points of ours. For instance, if one of us was down on his luck, out of work, flat broke, with no immediate help in sight, she would make sure to tell us about someone else's promotion at work, how much money she earned, how beautifully decorated her house was, or how great her marriage was.

She did not just tell you the news. She proliferated the details, repeated them at least ten times (which gave life to her purpose), and twisted and turned the invisible knife into the wounds of our inferior selves.

You might be wondering why this should bother anyone. It bothered us because, at the time, we were not emotionally strong enough to feel good about ourselves, and so our family conversations were more like individual and group threats. They felt more like personal attacks—insidious assaults on our psyches and covert censures of our fragile hearts. We didn't know it was more about her insecurity than it was about ours.

For years, she would take us apart and blow us to bits without realizing the consequences of her stormy battles. She was an army of one, powerful and omnipresent with her weapons of mass destruction that ignited ubiquitous toxic fumes. (You might know some people like this.)

After eighty-six years of battle, she surrendered and retreated into the quiet abyss of the condo she loved, where, thank goodness, she lived well—until cancer spread like wildfire throughout her emaciated, skeletal body in just five short months.

For having been at war for most of her life, at the end, she was a true soldier, brave and courageous during a losing battle with the most insidious of all diseases.

Suffering from the intolerable pain of chemotherapy and radiation and dying slowly from starvation, she never once complained about the magnitude of what she was going through. Cancer is the worst of all diseases, in my opinion.

If you knew my mother, this behavior defined who she was. She never complained about serious setbacks—the life-altering events she faced, like abject poverty, major illness, homelessness, and emotional bankruptcy. She worried more about wasting water and electricity and throwing away scraps of food.

Two

THE POWER OF YOU

My mother was at her best when she was telling us what we lacked or what we had done wrong. It seemed as though all her sentences began with the word "you."

The one I remember best is "You don't call me." This sentence was a powerful control tool! And it was so inaccurate because I called my mother almost every day. Hard to believe, right?

This four-word, passive-aggressive sentence helps to explain the lack of self-awareness people have; it's a great example of how we see only ourselves in a relationship. My mother addressed only her own needs. It never dawned on her that she could pick up the phone and call me. Her waiting was the control mechanism. And me? I never saw the possibility of sharing the responsibility of keeping in touch. I blindly accepted complete control of the schedule.

For years, I responded with more frequent phone calls until one day I realized that my mother never called *me*. I remember the moment vividly. A light went on in my head. A voice whispered, "Why are you doing all the calling?"

Finally, I discussed this with my mother, and she actually did say, "Huh, okay, I never thought of that. I guess I could pick up the phone."

She did not see her role in any of the dysfunction. With a keen, disapproving eye, she saw only the flaws in others. It never dawned on her that she was half of any relationship.

She had to talk, whether or not you were ready to listen, especially if she felt bad because of something that had happened, even if she was not involved. She had to make her point because hers was the only one that mattered.

She could not manage her emotions, and there were always upheavals of great magnitude. She was not aware of how another person might feel. If we mentioned the possibility of another point of view, she quickly dismissed the notion that anyone else could feel anything at all. It was all about her. Our job was to calm her mania, soothe her discomfort, and placate her anger.

Adeline Moore

I think back on all the time we wasted trying to make her happy, to erase her sadness, to make up for her disappointments, to fill a void in her empty self, or to make her smile. Most of the time, our relentless, pathetic efforts were never enough. We were told what was wrong with us or someone else or with the event, the circumstances, the distance traveled, or any other detail of whatever venture we were involved in.

Three

GUARD YOUR VULNERABILITY

I realize that my effort to keep her steady stemmed from my need to make her see me. *Me!* Who I was. What I wanted and needed in our relationship, what might make me happy. What I had lost. What I was looking for and couldn't find. What I was worth. I wanted some validation of my identity. I wanted her to look into my heart and soul, which is something she could never do.

At the time, I had no idea what self-awareness was or that both my mother and I were emotionally deprived.

For years, I didn't know I could be entitled to half of a relationship or that I could expect any type of emotional affirmation in return. The thought never occurred to me because I didn't know what that meant. Looking back, I remember feeling awful after most of my interactions with my parents, but I never knew exactly why. *They never knew why, either.*

Ragged and haggard, we let others drain us until we have nothing more to give, and we don't know it. This is a terrible place to be. We are alive but barely. We show up physically, but we are not present. We are not available, accessible, reachable. Usually, the people we are with aren't, either.

We don't recognize the symptoms of emotional starvation. The deprivation is not quantitative and therefore not measurable. It's visible only to those who can recognize it: mentors who can help and perpetrators who want to feed on the cancer.

We, the emotionally hungry, have similar symptoms to those of the physically anorexic.

Over time, we lose vibrancy and the ability to thrive. We might become more introverted, or we might lash out in anger. We can't see our mirror image. We can't recognize ourselves. We don't even know what to look for. We are not aware. We think negative thoughts. We are never good enough. Tragedy abounds because our growth is stunted, and there's no one around to provide the nourishment to sustain us.

Emotional stability is the goal. We need to become infused with enough emotional strength so that we can catch up to where we are supposed to be.

Blind Sight

As they say in the medical community, we must first become stable before we can be released to live a normal life.

After we become stable, we have to be able to maintain the new level of expectation and interaction in our relationships. We must redefine ourselves.

Then we must redefine our relationships.

Expect some pushback when the new you emerges. People won't expect the *fortified* you. Interestingly, some won't know how to respond—especially the bullies.

Stand your ground. It will feel good to be empowered. Don't let anyone shake your confidence. Don't let anyone cause you to rethink what you know to be true. Hold close your own truths. They are yours alone. No one can take them from you, so don't let go of them. Hang on tightly!

Importantly, you must have as clear a view of yourself as you can possibly have. It's one thing to *say* you are emotionally stable; it's another thing to prove it to yourself. Be clear about the fact that your actions and behavior match your words and your thoughts. If they don't, then you are not ready to put yourself out there. Always guard your vulnerability with people you cannot trust.

Realistically speaking, we will always have encounters in which our emotional stability is tested. Life is not without challenges, no matter how healthy we become. And because we are human, we can never be perfect. There will be setbacks—reactions we would like to forget, responses we cannot take back.

But if you find yourself in too many of these scenarios, don't look at the people or circumstances. Keep working on getting a clearer view of yourself. It's always a good idea to talk to a professional if you are having trouble coping.

The whole world changes when you become emotionally fortified. You come to believe in yourself. You are comfortable with your own convictions. And if everything aligns as it should, you will have acquired enough humility to know that it's okay when someone doesn't agree with you. It's okay that someone has a different opinion—even someone you love.

You will feel the difference when you are centered with both feet planted.

You will have the strength to set your own path, and you will be motivated to follow it. You will enjoy your choices. You can exhale because you don't have to please anyone else to the point of losing yourself in the process.

You will have an identity, and you will like it. Sometimes, it's hard work to maintain new behavior, but it won't be long before you can look back and see your old self clearly…amazed that you couldn't see it before. The age-old question of "What was I thinking?" takes on new meaning. You pay homage to its philosophy.

The new view is startling at first.

The awakening is enthralling. You know where you've been. You know you will never go back. The gift is that you *can't* go back. It becomes an impossibility. You know you will be able to give at your choosing. You say when. You say how. You say to whom.

The boundaries of your invisible fences will be clear to everyone around you, especially the emotional bullies in your life. I'm not defending their pervasive, cantankerous ways. Keep in mind that some bullying may not be purposeful. Some bullying happens naturally because of the pathetic state we are in when we are emotionally malnourished. We feed off someone else's strength. This is a subconscious need we have. The bully has the same need—but in reverse. His or her emotional deprivation causes the taking in the relationship.

I'm guessing there are some bullies out there who are not aware that they are slowly killing others—innocently. They are parasites, living off our waning energy, sucking our emotional blood.

Four

Rumors and Gossip

There was no such thing as telling my mother something and not having it repeated, even if she knew it would hurt the person in question. She did not have the emotional strength or think enough of herself to hold information. This was a debilitating side effect of her crippling immaturity.

If we told her something in confidence, we would hear about it from someone else. If we felt sad or depressed or afraid or sensitive or disappointed or anxious, we would definitely feel worse after we talked to her. This type of conversation, where there was doom and gloom or gossip about someone in the family, would evoke her supernatural emotional energy. She could talk and smoke cigarettes for days on end.

Typically, several family members would get involved, on the telephone, screaming and yelling, crying hysterically, begging her to stop because someone had said something to somebody that was exaggerated, untrue, ugly, painfully true, shameful, hurtful, insulting, degrading, demeaning, or downright cruel.

There was no end to the emotional suffering, no shelter from this harsh, horrific, insidious storm. It would last for three to five days with no relief from our own misery and no escape from hers. My mother was tortured in every way and had a totally negative orientation. And she wasn't finished with us until everyone was suffering from the most severe emotional indigestion and choking on our own malignant familial reflux. The fallout was combustible, stamping its environmental footprint on our unsustainable, empty emotional landfills.

What hurt the most was that the innocent trust a child has in her mother was violated and diminished in importance. In other words, we would be emotionally destroyed when she used our very own vulnerability against us. She threw our weaknesses right back at us, and it felt awful. The worst feeling was when she made fun of our weaknesses like no one else could.

For instance, we weren't allowed to be sensitive—to feel good or bad about anything—if you can imagine that. If we felt sad, glad, happy, joyful, surprised, angry, disgusted, disappointed, frustrated, or afraid, she would dismiss our feelings and thereby invalidate the reality of our experience. We weren't entitled to feel the everyday emotions of everyday life.

Yet, my mother was in a bad mood and angry for most of her life. Only she was allowed to feel the emotions and display them in one solo performance after another. She owned the stage. We were the captive audience. We paid the costly price of admission.

We didn't know how much she was suffering. She didn't know how much it cost her to put on the show.

We had no vaccine against this incurable disease and no armor to put on. Sadly, we didn't even know we needed it.

We didn't know we were prisoners locked up in invisible chains. And, pathetically, it never dawned on us that we could set ourselves free.

In the beginning, we were too young to escape—and by *escape*, I don't mean moving away or severing a relationship. I don't believe in estrangement. It's the easy way out, an exit strategy chosen only by the weak.

I know many people who believe in this strategy, which suggests that the solution to all our problems is to run away. With this action plan and the fact that you cannot keep problems from coming, do you keep running for the rest of your life? Where do you run? Along what path? Who goes with you?

> *Never cut what you can untie.*
> *—Joseph Joubert*

The people I know who took this path do not seem to be any better off than those who stuck with their difficult situations. In fact, those who took the escape route are still talking about themselves and still telling others what to do. They are not free!

They missed the most important aspect of the awakening project, and that is that when you are free, when you do find yourself, you have nothing to run from, and you don't have much to say about it out loud. You can manage people, whether you like them or not, whether they agree with you or not, and whether they have hurt you or not. You learn to get over yourself and your own importance. You learn to get out of your own way.

This is the big reveal. I'm continually mystified by all those who miss this little gold nugget of truth.

It's us—not them.

Who knew at that time that the change would have to come from us? There was no one around to teach us how to get strong and resilient, and it's apparent none of us was hardwired that way.

We didn't know that the answers we needed were an arm's length away, inside our own psyches. All we had to do was find the tools to tap into them.

Five

DON'T EXPECT TOO MUCH

"Mom, why do you expect your neighbor to respond with more than a brief expression of sympathy?"

"She's all wrapped up in herself," my mother answers with frustration.

"But she doesn't know your history. There's no way she can understand your life story. You're expecting too much. Just let it go."

"I can't. I was there for her when she had her surgery. I was interested to know why she had no family support when she got sick."

"I know that about you. You do show a keen interest in others, and you listen to details. I do believe you care—but only to a point."

"What do you mean by that?"

"I mean you ask questions and respond, but those emotions don't stay with you. And if you are disappointed by how people respond to you, try not to share so much about yourself. Don't expect too much from others. Rely only on people you are close with when it comes to making yourself vulnerable and opening yourself up to trust."

"I can't be like that."

"Yes, you can. You must because your transparent style has brought you too much frustration and too many letdowns."

"Oh my goodness, how do you know that?"

"I know that we cannot expect anyone to totally grasp what we are saying, especially when what we're saying is in-depth and personal. There are only a few people who are willing to invest time in hearing your story. And without listening intently to what you are saying—which, by the way, would take you about six months to articulate—there's no way anyone could respond to you in the way you would like. It just doesn't work that way.

"Sometimes, in our moments of deep emotional turmoil, we reach out to another person, hoping he or she will respond with heartfelt interest and sincerity. But try, for a moment, to put yourself in the other person's place.

"Do a role reversal. Ask yourself how you feel when a neighbor or casual friend tells you something about her life or the lives of her loved ones.

"I know you respond in kind. But do you take it to heart? You know, as we talk about this, I realize that sometimes, you probably do.

"Mom, try to keep your emotions intact. Live with being uncomfortable for a few moments, a few hours, until you are able to talk about your feelings with the right person—someone who cares about you—but most important, someone who knows your history.

"Get in touch with how you feel when someone shares bad news with you.

"Unless it's a family member, someone you love, or a dear, close friend, I'm sure you don't internalize it in the same way. Unfortunately, most people don't have empathy, which means they cannot see things through another person's eyes. They cannot know what it's like to be you. Sympathy is a lot easier. People can express emotions they themselves feel or can identify with.

"And even then, they will hear bad news and respond with a similar story or experience about themselves.

"That's the way most people communicate. Not much we can do to change it except to realize we should pick and choose our audience.

Don't have too many expectations. Get a better grip on your own emotions and learn how to manage them. Guard your vulnerability."

Behave so as to eliminate control.

Six

MIRROR MIRROR OFF THE WALL

Sometimes, when you're bullied and insecure, you have impaired insight into your own self-worth. You get lost in trying to find happiness in pleasing others.

You look for validation from someone who is slowly trying to destroy you—and succeeding at it.

You begin to feel sick while the predator feels better. The session doesn't end until the dyadic dance is over. You are the lifeline for an emotional vampire.

"What do you mean, you lost the five dollars I gave you?" my mother screamed as she lunged at me, and her hand stung my cheek. "We need milk and bread. Now what are we supposed to do? You're so stupid. I can't ask you to do anything." (Was this a learned response mechanism my mother had acquired?)

I was five years old when this happened. I must have dropped the money as I walked from our apartment in the projects to the Key Food grocery store, which was a few miles away.

I remember when I was swinging on a chain-link rope and fell back and hit my head on the concrete edging. I was bleeding and crying. My mother was so angry. She hit me and screamed—telling me I was so stupid for falling.

She went to get her friend, Virginia, who nursed the nasty gash I had on the back of my six-year-old skull. My mother absolutely did not have time for illness or injury of any kind. It made her crazy. I had no idea why at the time.

Seven

Reprieve

Amid the turmoil, there was respite in the escape visits to my grandmother's house. My grandmother loved me unconditionally, and I knew it at an early age. I often think—in fact, I know—that she saved me.

The funny thing is, my grandmother spent two years in a mental institution and had shock treatment with insulin, a barbaric method used to treat "mental illness" in the 1930s and '40s. I remember the family saying she was delusional, irrational, and unable to cope. At the time, I wasn't aware of her disabilities. All I knew is what I felt and what I saw.

No one realized that my grandmother suffered from trichotillomania, which, according to WebMD, is a condition characterized by "an irresistible urge that people have to pull out their hair, usually from their scalp, eyelashes and eyebrows."

This explains a lot. I remember how my grandmother had wisps of wiry, wavy gray hair that framed her hairline and face—just enough hair to peek through the tightly knotted kerchief she wore every time we went out. This doesn't make sense to me—we'd have to sit in the front row at the movie theater because my grandmother refused to wear eyeglasses. She was too vain to wear glasses but not to be bald at forty-five years old.

Vanity is the quicksand of reason.
—George Sand

She took care of me physically and emotionally. I felt safe and loved. We went all over Brooklyn—on foot, by bus, by train, and by trolley to Radio City, the Roxy Theatre, Eighteenth Avenue, Fort Hamilton Parkway, the Forty-sixth Street Loews, and other neighborhood hangouts. She bought me my first egg cream and my first training bra. She made sure I had a decent pair of shoes. She told me that I was special and that someday, I would marry a prince.

Eight

Self Talk

These conversations were totally different from any I had with my mother.

In fact, I cannot remember too many good conversations with my mother until I was about forty. She began to need me to take care of some things that were going on with my siblings, and she began to enjoy her grandchildren.

She began to enjoy me in the way we might enjoy pull-through advertising. But I knew deep down that it wasn't really me she enjoyed. I was a body…some body…somebody who filled a big void in her tumultuous life.

I said this to her throughout the years, and she fiercely denied it. I commented on her narcissism, and she angrily objected.

"I hate being the center of attention," she'd say. "I don't look at myself in the mirror all day." Or "What are you talking about? I'm totally the opposite of that," she'd scream.

Oh, how I hated the malignant self-love!

"But Ma, if that's true, why do you always act out when we socialize? Why do you insist on steering the conversation in one direction? Why do you want to talk only about your life and how much you suffered? Why do you publicly fight with Dad, if you're not focused on yourself?"

It was clear to me, after a ten-year conversation on the subject, that she absolutely could not grasp the concept. I understood that it was beyond her reach and she couldn't be fixed. The damage was irrevocable, deep in her psyche, and she could not go back to being the eight-year-old little girl who owned the voice in her head.

But may the God of all Grace, who called us to His eternal glory by Jesus Christ, after you have suffered awhile—perfect, establish, strengthen and settle you.
—1 Pet. 5:10

Nine

Exit Signs

We paid for this deficiency. We paid dearly, each of us in different ways. Some of us became caretakers and caregivers. We numbed the pain with whatever we could substitute for emotional nourishment. We lost ourselves in the false hope of a miracle that would never happen.

We spent time trying to solve problems that weren't ours. We wasted years trying to help those who didn't know they had to help themselves. We didn't know it, either. We had the right to detach, but this never occurred to us.

Detachment was not in our realm of thinking, not part of the enmeshed world we lived in. No one knew very much at all. We were socialized into and by our own immediate, normal environment.

Our ways became the normal ways of doing things, of living life, of thinking and behaving. It never occurred to us that there was another way of doing something or, more importantly, a different way to respond. We didn't know what we were entitled to.

Our emotional state was our enemy. We were too weak to move naturally from one stage to another. We did not develop properly. Chronologically, we moved from one age to the next, but emotionally we stopped growing when the trauma started.

So here we were, children in adult bodies—and what an ugly sight. We couldn't see the situation clearly enough and early enough in our emotional development.

Lack of self-awareness is the worst thing that happened to us. It stunted our emotional growth, and we walked around in circles. The circles got bigger, but we remained the same size. Without an exit strategy, we settled on a treadmill.

We cycle in the ride of our lives—in a downward spiral—without being able to see a different path, blindsided by our own inability to see there are exits in the circle.

Ten

LIFE AFTER DEATH

Maybe I did more for my mother out of a sense of responsibility than for any other reason; I'm not sure. But now I know I was looking for something I was never going to find.

My mother had the opportunity to tell me how she felt. I spent a lot of time with her, hours at a time, a few days a week, after she was diagnosed with terminal esophageal cancer. My siblings and I brought her food, took her to her doctors' appointments, did her laundry, kept up with paperwork, telephoned family members, cleaned the house, paid the bills, did errands, kept her clean, changed her sheets, and bought her new clothes because she had lost so much weight.

I sat by her sickbed and soothed her with comforting words. I brushed her hair, did her nails, and massaged her hands and feet.

I asked her how she felt about facing death. Was she ready? How did she feel about her life? How did she want to be remembered? What did she think her legacy was?

I realize now that nothing I could have done would have evoked the words a child wants to hear from her mother when her mother knows she is going to die in just a few months.

I imagine myself in that same scenario. What will I say to my children?

I will tell them how much I love them and appreciate all the memories we made together. I will thank them for making it possible for me to say, as a mother, hands down, that raising them was the most meaningful part of my life. I will remind them that I was not perfect and ask their forgiveness for my myopic vision when I should have had my eyes checked. I will want to hold their hands, to put my hands around each of their faces, to look at their strong bodies and their brilliant, creative minds and know that I helped to give life to these men.

Yes, I will make it clear that I love them unconditionally and that my life was rich and full because of them. They will know that nothing in this world was more precious or more important than they were.

I will be able to let go and die in peace. I will have said everything I wanted to say.

Me, at my mother's bedside? I wanted an apology. A heartfelt apology for the hurt that I suffered long before I was able to defend myself. I wanted to know how my own mother felt about me. Does this seem strange to you?

I understand that people have limitations. I also understand that post-traumatic stress disorder is not exclusive to military veterans. I am sure of that.

I understand that people cannot give what they do not have. I understand that we can't always fix damaged goods.

Eleven

Tunnel Vision

So what *is* there to understand? The fact that we stay in emotional bondage and subconsciously subject ourselves to continual rejection and hurt because of someone else's shortcomings?

Yes, we do. We do what we know best. We know our own normality, and we get comfortable. At the time of the trauma, we don't know that it's trauma. We don't even know that there is something wrong with the way we are living or that there is something different out there, another side to life or another way to live.

But in order to wake up from the nightmare, we need to get off the one-way street to see the oncoming traffic; otherwise, we'll only ever see what's in front of and alongside us. Without a different view, we cannot see what's coming toward us from the other side, and we definitely cannot see the various paths on which we could have taken our journeys.

As simple as it might sound, we need to experience something different, something better, something relatively close to normal—over and over and over again—until we begin to question our own normality. We must begin to realize exactly what we are entitled to and that life is different outside of the small world we once lived in. Somehow, we have to break free of the razor wire and the invisible steel chains of emotional bondage, the gripping vice of crippling codependency, the belts of anxiety that cinch our abundant waste. We need something transformative.

One-Way Street

You
With tunnel vision
Do you know who you are?
Your stare is so revealing,
But your eyes are so blind.

Can you imagine
For your whole life
You have looked only in one direction?

You travel on a one-way street
That stops at a dead end
Like one-sided relationships
That stop at a dead end.
The dead-end stops the one-way traffic.

The one-way traffic
Doesn't allow for a driver
On the other side of the road.

There may be fewer accidents,
But there are narrow passages and boring views:
No thoroughfare
No through traffic
No stop and go
No turns from oncoming traffic

Adeline Moore

No building
No expansion
No growth.

You never have to look out for the other person.

Good chance you will avoid a collision.
You will avoid gridlock.
You will avoid the view from the other side.

But we know how one-way, dead-end streets look over time.

The asphalt begins to crumble.
The grass grows too long.
The street becomes littered.
You might see some abandoned cars with their parts missing.

Twelve

MANHATTAN, 1930s

My father was wealthy as a child and dirt poor as a young adult. His father died when he was just fifteen, and his mother died when he was eighteen.

Though his life took him from privilege to poverty, he told us through the years how much he hated money, boarding school, and anything that resembled indulgence.

We didn't know why at the time. The story would unfold over the course of forty-three years (my lifetime with my father), one gloomy detail at a time.

First, my father's mother was addicted to sleeping pills (among other things), as the story goes. She couldn't get out of bed in the morning, and so my father missed a lot of school.

My grandfather's answer to this dilemma was to send my father away to military school. There my father would learn discipline and structure, just what an eight-year-old boy needed to fill the void of having parents who weren't available.

The problem was solved. He stayed there until he was fifteen, when his father died and somehow the family fortune mysteriously disappeared.

Thinking back, I wonder why my father hardly spoke about his parents, his privileged life, and his school experience. He would make random comments throughout the years, but there were no details or storytelling about his experiences. Surely, he must have had a lot to say because his life was anything but typical—definitely different from the lives his children were living.

We would have been interested to know more about his experiences.

Why did he keep the first eighteen years of his life a secret? With a beautiful mother and a wealthy, entrepreneurial father, he certainly would have had stories to tell.

Thirteen

Brooklyn, 1940s

My mother came from a poor family. Her parents separated when she was eight. My grandmother had a history of mental illness; my grandfather was weak and irresponsible with money. He didn't take care of his family. I don't remember seeing my grandfather more than three times in my entire life.

Because of this, my aunt and uncles and my parents and I—all seven of us—lived together with my grandmother for two and half years in her crowded two-bedroom apartment, which was located above a neighborhood bar. The bar attracted rats, which traveled through the cold-water pipes and plaster walls to visit us at night.

The windows of our apartment were a stone's throw from the "el"—the elevated train tracks that split through the avenue we lived on. The old, chalky-brown subway trains rumbled around the clock, shaking our windows as they came to a screeching halt—steel wheels on steel tracks—at the station.

The family grapevine says my grandmother suffered from delusions. I wasn't there; I can't say. But I wonder how much of her feeling of hopelessness came from having four children, no money, and no place to call home. Maybe she couldn't cope too well. In her defense, how many people could? As I said, I really don't know what happened when she had her alleged break from reality. I wasn't there. Or was I?

My mother was the oldest of my grandmother's four children and bore the brunt of most of the early trauma. She was the one who had to ask the neighborhood grocer if he could wait a few weeks to get paid for food they needed. She often slept with my grandmother as a young girl and would wake up when my grandfather came to the bedside, begging my grandmother to sleep with him.

My mother never asked for affection, especially from my father. She couldn't give affection too easily, either.

Then, when my mother turned sixteen, my grandmother decided my mother didn't have to finish high school. Instead, she sent her to business school to learn shorthand and typing so that my mother could quickly get a job and earn a paycheck.

My grandmother's brother paid the tuition, and my mother diligently went to business school, became a proficient typist and stenographer, and got an office job where she earned sixteen dollars a week—half of which she gave to my grandmother faithfully when she got paid.

It was 1946, the year my parents met. My mother said it was her one-way ticket out of her interrupted childhood.

My father was handsome and strong. He was smart and funny, with a terrific sense of humor. He was articulate and easy to talk to. My mother says she was drawn to him because he had charisma; he was like a magnetic force. But—magnetic lines of force do not intersect each other. They exist side by side, each aware of the other, unable to move too far away without feeling the pull.

My parents' relationship would evolve into a magnetic minefield—each one of them an individual magnet, one pointing north and one pointing south. With tremendous force and emotion, they were attracted to each other. Yet there were too many negative charges, and they lived their lives afraid to touch any of the connecting wires for fear of getting too close, getting burned, even though they felt the force of the magnets pulling them together.

They worked as ushers at the Winter Garden Theatre on Broadway, and often, after work, the crowd hung out at the automat and talked about the evening's performance and the famous people they had seen.

Adeline Moore

My father was head usher; my mother, an usherette who worked for him. There they were, nineteen and seventeen years old, standing in the dark, night after night, and then walking out into the "Great White Way" as their day began right after midnight.

They were immediately attracted to each other and found it easy to talk, which they often did until the lights went out on Broadway (literally). They found in each other a solace, a reprieve, a relief from their painful childhoods.

My mother's impoverished, humble beginnings and my father's wealthy, privileged lifestyle were all too similar in ways we would learn more about.

Their earlier surroundings were different, but their lives were the same. Both suffered from abandonment.

Nurturing was something unfamiliar to them. I wonder if either of them was ever held by anyone else but the other. And here they were, teenagers in Times Square, working in one of the busiest places on earth, the crossroads of the world, lost children who had found each other in an adult world, stuck to each other, even though everything else in their lives had come unglued.

Fourteen

Abandonment

At twelve, my mother knew the harsh, cold loneliness of a children's home. Cared for by nuns in a Catholic orphanage, she learned how to clean the old convent and church. Unknowingly uncomfortable in her own young skin, she learned to move in stiff, unforgiving communal clothing, pieces she had chosen from the heap of recycled rags that were piled high on top of the large wooden table in the orphanage—the daily fashion runway every young girl living there walked with feckless, reckless abandon. Her long, thick, naturally wavy hair was chopped off—scissored close to her head.

At eight, my father knew the harsh, cold loneliness of a military boarding school. Generals and colonels were his mentors, sensitive men who were responsive and attentive to a child's needs. He learned absolute obedience as he did his schoolwork stoically, soldier-like in his military school garb, which had also been recycled in the bin of collective uniformity. His straight, thick blond hair was careened and marined, shaved close to his head, hardly visible in the space between the unforgiving fabric of his stiff, peaked cap and the soft skin of his eight-year-old ears.

Coincidentally, my parents were both around eight years old when their lives began to unravel. (I see it now, how the devastation lasted throughout their lifetimes.) None of us really knew what had happened until it was over.

The only way I can picture my parents as teenagers in Times Square in 1946 is to think about old movies or photographs I've seen. I'm realizing as I write this that my mother would speak often about how handsome my father was, yet now I cannot remember him ever commenting on my mother's looks.

And, oh, was she stunning! A first-generation Italian American, she had flawless skin, defined cheekbones, big brown eyes, and thick, dark brown, naturally wavy hair—and she was petite at five foot two and 110 pounds. She was 1940s gorgeous.

I'm wondering why my father never described her, because he was so articulate, so good with words.

Some say my father looked a lot like President John F. Kennedy. I guess he did, although prejudicially, I say my dad was much more handsome. Yes, he had the thick wave of hair and clear blue Irish eyes, but his face was more angular, perfectly chiseled from high forehead to chin; his defined cheekbones drew a straight line to his jaw. Movie-star good looks.

Their loneliness and longing would remain as they buried their emotions for fear of rejection, a comfortable feeling they knew all too well. How could they step into the unfamiliar territory of trust and vulnerability?

I couldn't feel so I couldn't trust.
—Leonard Cohen

They married in April 1947, and although, subconsciously, they tried to bond with each other, the trauma of what was to come became an electrifying disconnect for the rest of their lives together.

Fifteen

The Tornado That Leveled Everything

In 1949, at the age of twenty-two, my father caught the polio virus and would never walk again without the help of braces and canes. His legs were paralyzed. My mother was twenty. I was two.

My father was hospitalized for six months, suffering through a horrible disease that ravaged his body, destroying nerves and muscles in both legs and leaving us—my mother and me—suffering...alone, afraid, hungry, and homeless.

Polio is a disease that runs its course and leaves its victims with varying effects. Each case is different in severity, the consequences of the disease ranging from small impairments, such as a slight weakness in one hand, to complete paralysis and/or death. My father's spinal cord was affected, so he lost the movement of both legs.

At the time of his death, forty years after he first got sick, his legs were skeletal. Literally, they were bones covered by a thin layer of mottled skin, miraculously holding up his heavier upper body. He had become dysmorphic.

We lost my father as we knew him, and we lost the promise of a better life. My mother knew that life would never be the same again. My father fought the truth. How much harder could it be? How much harder would it get?

He had a bad case of the dreadful disease, one that leaves you with half of your overall strength everywhere—not just in the affected body parts. Your nerves work twice as hard to do half as much. (I'm thinking about how disabled people are among our most marginalized, yet they complain the least of the oppressed.)

I don't think many people know what this type of oppression looks like. Because of media coverage, riots, picket lines, and collective outcries, other groups get a lot of attention—and yes, they deserve attention, believe me. Of course they do. But so do the disabled, who are all too often…forgotten and forlorn lost souls.

People stare. They are uncomfortable because disabled people might look different.

Sometimes their bodies are not perfectly formed; sometimes limbs are missing.

Sometimes they cannot speak; they struggle to get words out—to no avail.

Sometimes they shake; they cannot stop moving. Sometimes they cannot move; they are paralyzed and left with atrophied muscles and dead nerves, as my father was.

Some are fortunate to have family support; however, I remember my mother telling me how some women left their husbands when their husbands came down with polio. They couldn't deal with the stress that major illness brings.

We take so much for granted. Imagine not being able to walk—ever again.

I remember the long stares from people walking past us on the streets of Brooklyn in the early 1950s. I remember the looks of astonishment, surprise, intrigue, curiosity, pity, indifference, and, believe it or not, *fear* pasted on their squeamish faces—the universal expressions of emotion twisted in wrinkled confusion, sometimes disbelief, at what they were seeing. Were their subconscious calls for help answered with detailed explanations of what had happened to this person who had been put on display for all the world to see?

Why do we always expect what's normal?

My father had a fierce pride that kept him from sitting in a wheelchair, where he should have been his whole life because it would have kept him safe. He wouldn't have fallen as much as he did. I remember he slipped on a marble floor in the lobby of a New York City skyscraper and split his head open.

I think he knew that life would look different from a sitting position. Somehow he knew that he would always be looking up at other people and would never see them eye to eye—a perspective that would change how he interacted with others. People would look at him differently: maybe with pity, maybe with fear of the unknown, maybe with some level of discomfort.

Often, people don't know how to act when someone is different from them. They might pay more attention to a person pushing a wheelchair than to the person in the wheelchair because the person pushing is, in their eyes, "normal."

Also, knowing my father, I believe he didn't want to be thought of as different, even though he was, by standard definitions of the word. But again, who defines "normal?" Who determines how we should look at someone if he or she doesn't fit our preconceived notion of how things should look? It's scary how much importance we place on ourselves, isn't it?

Anyway, experts say that eye contact is the most important non-verbal skill and the single most important factor in establishing human connection. So I'm assuming that life is different if you cannot make eye contact that easily. There must be some sort of adjustment both people have to make, and by then a lot of time has passed, so you miss the initial spontaneity of first impressions.

So instead of looking up at others from waist level and a somewhat comfortable sitting position, my father chose instead to live dangerously with every compromised step he took. Risk outweighed loss.

We look back on his life and cannot believe what he accomplished in his physical condition. Truthfully, it's mind-boggling. And it's unfortunate for me that I learned so much so late in my life, like the fact that my father's illness was such a good example of how clueless people are. How you can tell your story except to a handful of people?

Unfortunately, my father's history provides yet another example of how we cannot expect too much from others. There's no way we can tell our story so that others will understand. There's no way we can tell it so that they will want to. In a five-minute conversation, you might get an "Oh, gee, that must have been hard," or "That's just like what happened to my cousin. He broke his foot and couldn't walk for six weeks."

> *"Dad, I think you expected too much. You gave people too much credit."*

The emotional baggage my parents carried was heavy enough and weighed them down—long before the tragedy of devastating illness and the forthcoming infinite hardship. The three of us faced a daunting reality. Life was hard from that point on.

> *You never get everything in life.*
> *You should like what you get.*
> *Say good-bye to getting what you like.*

Sixteen

BROOKLYN, 1950s

With nowhere to live after my father was discharged from his six-month hospital stay, we found housing in Canarsie, Brooklyn, in the government-built Quonset Huts. These mezzaluna dwellings accommodated people after the World War II housing shortage. They were small and crescent shaped, with porches attached to their half-moon, horizontal steel faces.

My mother says she was happy there even though we were poor, underserved, underprivileged, disadvantaged, disenfranchised, and, sadly—something that would never change—disabled. We were part of "the lost, the last, the least," the left-out and lonely population of society's most marginalized.

Our little house was small and clean and served our needs. My sister was born there. So now we were a family of four: my father, recovering from polio, unsure and afraid about how he would make his way in the world; my mother, resolved to homemaking—unhappy and complaining, probably wondering how she was going to manage every physical aspect of our lives by herself.

Me? I had a sister, and even though I was only four when she was born, I knew what it felt like to love someone more than I loved myself. Funnily enough, with all the hardship and heartache, my parents were also ecstatic over the birth of their second little girl.

Two years earlier, when I was two and my father was in the hospital with polio, my mother had given birth to a stillborn son. So my sister's birth was planned and welcomed.

My mother didn't realize it at the time, but my father's illness took its toll on all aspects of our lives. She was just twenty years old, with a two-year-old daughter (me) and a sick husband who was hospitalized with an incurable disease, and she was already pregnant again with a second child. It is apparent that, with no fixed place to call home, and under the stress of visiting my father in the hospital, which required a long train ride every day, she became morbidly exhausted and weak, and that her exhaustion caused her to lose the baby, her tiny son.

Blind Sight

On the day before my mother died, she told my sister she was thinking about her six children. While we were planning my mother's funeral, my sister whispered to me, "Mom told me she had six children."

My sister says it made her realize our mother was close to the end of her life. Our mother had said she had six children. "My six children." Six—not five.

Her little boy who did not live was one of us. The six of us belonged to her.

Seventeen

UNTAPPED RESOURCES

My father took odd jobs, barely able to hobble around, unsteady on two small canes, selling women's clothing door to door in our small, barracks-like neighborhood. We were living in abject poverty. I can't remember anything about food in my early years, but I remember I was always hungry.

I was outdoors a lot, on my own, at two and a half years old. My mother kept the door locked so I couldn't go inside while she was having coffee with her friends.

When I was much older, I asked my mother why she and my father never received any type of help with food, housekeeping, child care, physical therapy, and mental health. Did they have support groups for people with major illness and disease, permanent disability, a history of stillbirth, abandonment, lack of education and job skills, institutionalization, long-term hospitalization, homelessness, and poverty?

I realize more and more why we children never complained about anything.

No one had time for pain of any kind, and for some reason, no one ever got sick. It's one of our collective small family miracles. How could my parents have taken care of sick children when they were already running on empty in full survival mode? They could not have endured the added burden of needing more resources.

Resources and help? I can tell you unequivocally that no one ever so much as gave these ideas a thought.

Eighteen

Brooklyn, 1950s
Concrete Walls and Tenement Halls

In the early 1950s, we moved from the Quonset Huts to a low-income housing project because we needed a place to live. The huts were being torn down, and my father was still recovering from polio.

What can I say about living in such a place? What image does it conjure up if you've never lived in one? I will do my best to describe it as accurately as I can.

It's been sixty-five years, and the memories are bad.

For one thing, we were surrounded by large families living in small apartments—in cramped spaces framed in cement cinder block, oxidized iron, and painted steel.

I remember how these poor families moved in groups. I guess they had to because there wasn't enough room to breathe. They desperately needed to bathe and wash their hair, which I remember always looked stringy and damp.

Fortunately, one of my mother's most redeeming qualities was her ability to keep an immaculate home and take care of our physical needs at the same time. She kept our apartment as clean as she kept the Quonset hut. Literally, you could eat off the floor. My father could not help around the house at all, and my sister and I were too young. This was one of the many ways in which my mother was amazing. She was efficient, clean, and organized.

Money is no guarantee of a perfect life. But you cannot afford to be poor. You begin with such a deficit, and you spend so much time trying to catch up—time that middle-class people spend on more normal things like planning a life with job security, adequate housing, food and clothing, visits to the dentist, pride, self-confidence, security, less stress, and a healthier self-image.

Poverty is poverty. It knows no particular ethnicity, skin color, or language.

Poor people look at the world differently. You walk around with a concave chest and a deflated ego, knowing you are different from other people—if you're lucky enough to see other people—because when you're poor, you live in a minuscule world.

Poverty has a universal face with empty eyes, a hopeless spirit, a lack of awareness, and limited access to anything beyond the length of your own arms.

The poor do not travel far outside of their invisible binding perimeters.

We surely didn't. Housing projects were home to us and others with a multitude of problems besides poverty, such as unemployment, lack of education and vocational skills, lack of resources, and a wide range of other social problems.

We didn't see flowers, plants, or trees. They were not part of our world. I never saw a suburban residential community until I was thirteen.

And because of our lack of self-awareness and social skills, we failed to see at the time how our surroundings probably added to our low levels of self-esteem and confidence. My mother's words echo in my ears.

"I always felt inferior. I had no confidence."

As a family, we had no money, so, of course, we had no car. Because my parents were teenagers when they got married, they never finished high school or college. They surely didn't have a lot of earning power.

During the years of our abject poverty, my father thought of going to college to prepare himself for the workforce. He was physically

Blind Sight

disabled, so there was no way he could ever have earned a living doing manual labor. Also, he always wanted to be a sports writer for the *Daily News*, but that, too, could never have happened because he would never have been able to handle the logistics of a job like that.

So he decided to finish high school and then apply to Brooklyn College to earn a degree in English, which he did in 1959 (at night) while he worked full time and was a husband and a father of three young daughters. And, as we had no car, he rode to college on the subway, lifting one leg at a time from step to step as he climbed the long, dirty, underground tiled stairways of the New York City Transit Authority.

After years of rehabilitating himself, regaining some strength, and learning how to get around on two canes and braces, my father barely got on his feet (literally) and found a job in Manhattan. He had to walk to the bus stop, which was at least two miles from the front door of our apartment building.

A few years ago, sixty years after all of this took place, my husband and I took a trip into Brooklyn because he wanted to see where I was born and where I grew up. I realized, as we stood there together on a cold December day in 2014, just how far my father had walked to the bus stop.

How on earth did he walk that far? This was another one of our collective family miracles, because if you had seen the condition he was in and how far he walked, you'd say I was lying. I'm not. It's true. But how did he do it?

"Dad, help me to see this. Maybe I can understand the will to do it; maybe I can understand your determination and perseverance—but actually, how did you manage the treacherous balancing act?" My heart hurts.

"Why did you do it? For us? For yourself? For the preservation of your own dignity and self-respect? Did you do the impossible to fool yourself into thinking that you could live a normal life? Did you refuse help because of pride or because of fear? Did you refuse to accept what happened? Did you think about asking for help? I'm thinking it never even occurred to you.

"The truth is you were not like everyone else. You didn't have to be. That's the part you missed. In your fight to ignore what happened to you, to not let your disease define you, you lost sight of the fact that you were quite extraordinary and unique—not like anyone else indeed. Hardly! You didn't have to be.

"Dad, you had confidence as people stared you down. You were a warrior in the fight of your life. But your blind spot prevented you from seeing yourself. This was the worst of what happened to you.

"Somehow, you had the mental and physical strength to work, go to college, and take care of your family, but you had no emotional strength to take care of yourself. I don't think you knew how. Did you feel the abandonment and recognize it? Or was it buried so deeply inside of you that the emptiness filled you up?

"How could you breathe, carrying such a heavy load, swallowing your fear every minute of every day with every shaky step you took? One wrong move and you were flat on your back. Just the fact that you needed a lot of space around your walking area because of your outstretched arms and pointed canes makes me wonder how you were able to take two steps without falling.

"Did you begin every day with the reality that you couldn't move your legs? Do you remember the simple task of getting out of bed every day, lifting up one leg at a time?

"And by the time you got dressed and somehow out the door and somehow onto the bus and somehow to the office—did you wonder how you got there? Did you wonder if anyone else could imagine what you were carrying or understand what it was like to have no one carrying you? There was no help anywhere. Did you wonder about that?

"What did the discrimination feel like? What was it like to see the awkward surprise on people's faces when you showed up for an interview, falling hard into a chair because you could not bend your knees and balance yourself enough to just sit down like the rest of us can? Your résumé did not reveal your physical disability. On paper, where the words flowed, no one knew you couldn't walk."

Adeline Moore

Facework

Keep your dignity
In every interaction
You say
A tall order
The desire to rescue
A sacred respect
For ourselves
And others

Bias
Preconceived notions
Stereotypes
Eliminate control
As a goal
Face work
Mutual understanding
In the purest sense
How do I?

Nineteen

REVELATION

I am not angry, and I know why. I am not one of those people who spend their whole lives blaming others for what they didn't get. I took the journey to find myself. And I would never articulate, as so many people do, the overused phrase "I am in a good place." Maybe I am. Maybe I'm not. If I am, who says so? If I'm not, who says so? Who determines the verdict? Whom is it according to?

Don't let anyone tell you where you are! And make sure that the place you describe for yourself is accurate. If not, you will find out soon enough that you have to navigate your way in the right direction—wherever that turns out to be!

I find that most people who say this don't even know where they are, and more importantly, if they were in a good place, they wouldn't have to say it out loud to others.

It's easy enough for people to see where we are.

Believe It

Leave it to me
Leave me
Let it be
Achievement

Bring it to me
Bring me back
So it is
Retrieve Meant

Climb the stairs
Climb up
Rise above
The Ease Meant

Twenty

Lost and Found

*P*eople try to find themselves in strange ways. *A good place. A bad place.*

What do these words even mean? Truthfully, we don't have to look too far to see our own selves—if we know that we are looking—and if we really want to see the cold, hard facts of who we are.

We can tap into our own reality if we stop looking at others and to others for answers we will not get and for things we are missing. What we are missing can be found in the depths of our experiences, which can be found inside of our own heads, hearts, minds, and souls.

To make room for these fresh, new gifts, we have to clean the well of toxic thoughts that may have seeped in from contaminated sources over the years.

We have to ferret out the maligned mirror image.

Mirror, mirror off the wall.

Be ready to see an unobstructed view of your own life. You have to be able to see yourself so clearly and be humble enough to go the distance when you do not like what you see. Put yourself out there and become vulnerable. Now add some humility to the mix. Swallow hard and be ready and willing to accept the consequences of acceptance and rejection so that you don't cave in.

In fact, run so hard into yourself that you shatter the mold into a million pieces.

If you do this, you will not ever be able to put the pieces back together again because the original cast will be gone.

Your untapped self will no longer exist.

Stay above the fray. It's damned hard to tread water for a long time. It's a risky investment, but the payoff is huge. You will pass Go freely. You will never go to jail, imprisoned by your own self-induced gripping fear, letting others take ownership of the right to be true to yourself. Listen only to your own voice.

I learned this by watching my parents self-destruct because of low self-esteem, poor self-image, muddled identity, and debilitating insecurity. True, they had good reason to feel hopeless.

But I can see more clearly now that despite all their major, life-altering setbacks, the worst thing that happened to them was that they lacked emotional nourishment and strength. This starvation left exposed, opened, unprotected, ulcerated wounds that formed a maze of scars on their wind-broken hearts.

Scared, they let fear take over their lives. It kept them from trusting. It took away all hope of a better life. It paralyzed them emotionally.

They could never get the words out—the ones they needed to hear to be free.

Twenty-One

CHARACTER AMONG CHARACTERS

My parents were characters in a melodrama. They were complex protagonists whose most redeeming quality was character.

They say you can tell how much character someone has by how he or she handles power. That might be true—it probably is. But character is also about managing setbacks, those life-altering events that change the course of your life but don't leave you feeling sorry for yourself. That's a good look at character.

With all that we missed because of hardship, somehow our parents were able to give us values and beliefs that would set us on a path toward hard work and understanding of the human condition. All of us believed all people were the same; we had the gift of empathy. We were good listeners. We were generous and altruistic. We were not ignorant. And we have never hosted a pity party.

My parents did not think the world owed them anything, but maybe we children paid for what they did not get. That's the tragedy. You must get the help you need. Symptoms mean something. They cannot go untreated. Just as we need medicine for any physical disease, we needed help for our emotional disease.

Unfortunately, emotional illness is sometimes lumped in with and treated as mental illness, which has a more profound effect on self-fulfilling prophecy.

A mental illness diagnosis is given too easily and too frequently because some don't understand the human suffering that is born purely from emotional illness and deprivation that do not have a mental illness component. I was always disappointed when I went for therapy because I never got the help I needed.

And believe it or not, my mother went for therapy also (later in her life), and not one therapist recognized that the unfixable, broken pieces of her life were the result of morbidly acute emotional starvation—emotional malnutrition.

In fact, two weeks before my father died, a therapist came to my parents' house to conduct an intervention with our biological family, my parents and their five children. (Yes, after all the setbacks and life-altering events they suffered, my parents went on to have five children.)

The intervention was a disaster! The therapist had no idea what she was dealing with and, tragically, did not have the experience to treat emotional illness.

We were afraid—pure and simple!

Her approach exacerbated our already fragile states, and chaos ensued. I can recall the morbid details to a point, but not enough to articulate them so precisely.

I do remember, however, that we were yelling and crying. People were talking. No one was listening.

Things got out of control, and my father became frantic. He was desperate and could not get his emotions in check. He was engulfed in fear—fear of the future, fear of being retired and facing life every day with my mother, fear of not being able to take care of himself if they separated, and fear of not being able to take care of himself if they stayed together.

He knew he faced the rest of his life in hell, where his already-broken spirit would be hammered and shattered into a million little pieces.

My mother would become a larger emotional wrecking ball than she already was because now she would have her prey all to herself, twenty-four hours a day.

(Part of my father's fear was exacerbated by post-polio syndrome, which he didn't know he had at the time. Sadly, he died without ever knowing that the symptoms and effects of polio had returned forty years after he had first become infected with the virus.)

According to Daniel Wilson, Ph.D., "post-polio syndrome wears out your body parts. The return of old symptoms is psychologically and physiologically devastating. You are tired, running out of energy."[1] This is paralytic polio that has run its course, destroyed muscles and nerves, and now comes back to do more damage after lying dormant for four decades.

> *"The polio virus is not latent in the body; it's ingested in the mouth by polluted food and it affects nerves. Healthy nerves do double labor...supplying stimulation to muscles. But the healthy nerves start to malfunction and the affected person becomes exhausted. You believe you conquer polio but it comes back."*[2]

PPS gradually progresses. It's forever. It's never done.

> *"PPS does things to your body you don't realize. Maybe you don't want to admit you're losing more. Having polio complicates the*

---

[1] Daniel J. Wilson, *Living with Polio: The Epidemic and Its Survivors* (Chicago: Chicago University Press, 2005).

> *aging process. If you're weak, you think you want to exercise more. But it affects muscles and nerves. Nerves supply muscles. Nerve abuse makes malfunction worse. So exercising is out of the question. Rest is the only thing. There are no cures. Hundreds of thousands of survivors wonder what the future will hold."*[3]

Like a lot of survivors, my father wanted to put his illness behind him. But the overwhelming fatigue took control. I remember how frustrated he was because he didn't know what was wrong with him. He started to feel this way in his early sixties.

And like many other examples of a lack of awareness, how could it be that an intelligent, articulate, educated, well-read, informed person like my father would miss the fact that the life-altering disease he lived with for forty years came back to claim his life, to eat away at the little bit of energy he had left?

How did we miss this?

> *"There is no money for research on PPS. It's the only group that has to take care of itself. People must make others aware. Get vaccinated. There are thousands of PPS cases diagnosed each year. See your doctor."*[4]

Stampede

He said you were like a posse
Coming
'Round the bend
Tied to the chair
Word Strike!

Dumbstruck
Strung up
Last word
Unheard of

Daunting
Flaunting
Ability
Inability
Disability
Enabled
Dis
Abled

My father never again went home after the intervention. The emotional chaos and crippling anxiety caused him a trip to the emergency room of a local hospital, where he was admitted for two days and then transported directly to a mental health facility. He died there, two weeks later, at age sixty-three, of congestive heart failure.

Here was another example of how unchecked emotions can destroy us. My father was extremely intelligent. His cognitive ability was intact. He did not have a mental illness. Instead, he suffered from abandonment, insecurity, unresolved issues associated with getting polio, being orphaned and homeless at eighteen, and feeling trapped in an extremely dysfunctional relationship with my mother. Fear!

As a child, he was rich, well fed, alone, afraid, confused, and ill equipped to be on his own. As a teenager, he was poor, hungry, homeless, orphaned, alone, afraid, confused, and ill equipped to be on his own. As an adult, he was disabled, afraid, confused, and ill equipped to be on his own. He was part of society's most marginalized—in different ways—throughout his entire life.

Unfortunately, mental health professionals were not as aware as they are now of how our emotions affect our health. At the time, they were more concerned with cognitive intelligence and "mental illness," which they were trained to diagnose and label for insurance purposes. *Change the way you act, and you will change the way you feel.* Really?

What about getting in touch with how you feel, getting to the bottom of why you feel that way, figuring out where the feelings are coming from, and then finding a way to work through the wave of emotions you face when they are uncovered?

Then, learn how to feel uncomfortable for a while. Live with your own discomfort and the feeling of being unsettled. Realize these feelings are emotionally generated. Work hard at learning how to manage your emotions, how to control yourself, how to anticipate your own behavior. Learn how to manage this discomfort and know you must do it—no matter what. Learn how to control unwanted, unruly behavior. Respond, but don't react.

Then, figure out how and where you can find out how to feel good—happy, joyful, grateful, affirmed, acknowledged, respected, identified!

Otherwise you wind up feeling frustrated and not knowing why. Often, you are left with a hole in your heart that cannot be fixed with a Teflon patch.

This is what my parents experienced throughout their lives because they rode an emotional roller coaster. They were strapped in, going higher and higher, hearing the silent screams around them. They came crashing down time after time, coming to the unexpected abrupt halt, asking, "Is that it? Is that all there is?"

How can we find someone to teach us early on about the life skills that build confidence, increase self-esteem, improve self-image and identity, and help us find a way to feel positive emotions? To get better, we have to learn how to feel good. To feel good, we have to become emotionally strong and resilient. To acquire these attributes, we have to experience, in detail, the kind of growth that enables us to see life through open, aware, gentle, forgiving, and understanding eyes.

I will wager a bet that there is a wide population out there suffering from a lack of life skills and social skills that impedes emotional growth. This emotional deficit sets us on a course of stunted growth and debilitating internal gridlock that result from enormous blind spots through an opaque view.

We can live our whole lives blind.

Twenty-Two

CHILDREN TAKING CARE OF CHILDREN

How do you begin to feel good about yourself when you don't know what it feels like to be nurtured? Simple things like sitting at a dinner table with parents who are able to take care of you, who put your needs above their own, are as foreign as a train ride on the Orient Express.

There are millions of children who will never know what that feels like.

In scenarios where parents are self-absorbed because of stunted growth and/or other unfortunate life experiences, children can become devoid of emotion and numb out at an early age because early on, they are in total survival mode. Because they are basically on their own emotionally and starving to be nurtured, they are robbed of their innocence in emotional ways.

There are scenarios in which older children take care of younger siblings and somehow provide some emotional nourishment out of care and concern. But it's not quite the same as having two healthy, emotionally developed parents.

Then there are children taking care of children, as in the case of my parents. Chronologically young and emotionally undeveloped, they got caught in the quagmire of naïve, unadulterated love and the promise of blind, ignorant bliss. Come on, now. They acted out a predetermined script.

What are the ramifications of improper labeling and self-fulfilling prophecies to the emotional have-nots who are already living on the other side of the divide?

I do believe you can be mentally healthy, free of a diseased brain, but not feel good because you are emotionally unhealthy. There is an enormous difference between diseases of the brain and diseases of the mind and heart. Emotional deficiency can cause issues with codependency and all the fallout, consequences, and backlash that go with it.

Have you ever been told that you have an emotional disease or an emotional illness? Probably not!

Diseases of the brain are genetic, biological, and yes, psychosocial, but there is usually a physical component in the mix. Our emotions are more intangible and help to define how equipped we are to handle life's ups and downs. The brain can supply all the factual data in the world to help us make a decision. But our emotions will usually be the final decision makers and steer us in the direction we choose to take (based on how we feel).

Yes, it is true that if we don't develop properly, socially and emotionally, our stunted growth can affect us psychologically, which can affect our moods, which can affect our behavior. Then, when we begin to realize we are dying from thirst and drawing from an empty well, someone tells us that we need behavior modification therapy to learn how to cope in the world. This is a vicious cycle. A vicious circle.

Emotional strength lies more in the arena of self-awareness, self-care, self-esteem, self-confidence, self-knowledge, self-motivation, and self-identity. It is how we acquire the ability to control negative thoughts, regulate internal and external behaviors, and rein in some unstoppable destructive impulses.[5]

---

5 Daniel Goleman, *Emotional Intelligence: Why It Can Matter More Than IQ* (New York: Random House, 1995).

Twenty-Three

Listen and Listen Good: Don't Confuse Hearing with Listening

How do we get stronger? Where can we find this type of strength? Where is the cure for our zealous solicitude? We can find it in a few places.

But you must get out of your station. You must race against the wind.

Search for transformation. Navigate treacherously painful imbalance on your emotional surfboard. Get a foothold on the slippery surface of the war-torn, shattered, scattered fragments of your life.

It can be as simple as going to work and learning from colleagues. To do this, you have to work with great people. You have to stay quiet for a long time, with your eyes wide open. You have to forget about what you think you know and to soak in, like a sponge, all that you can possibly absorb—about life, about what you observe, about how people behave. Jump right in with both feet, give 100 percent of your energy, and learn to listen well. Make that your number-one priority. Speak less. Listen much more—with your ears, your brain, your eyes, and your heart. Leave your ego at the door.

This behavior is easier if you are young and at the beginning of your career. If you are somewhere in the middle but not able to get over the hump of mediocrity, get ready to humble yourself, and get ready to listen up. Put yourself back into student mode. Close your mouth. Open yourself to scrutiny.

This can be a life-altering experience. You will need to learn a lot about humility. Otherwise you will not be able to carry out this mission.

Another way for us to see the light is that we might get lucky to be mentored by a shepherd who knows that one of his or her sheep needs a little more help than the rest of the flock. He or she carries a large scepter. This person must be willing to invest the time; it must be someone selfless with nothing to gain but the reward of truly helping another person to lead a better, more fulfilling life. It's a lofty and noble goal. But, believe it or not, there are people like this out there. It's up to us to find them. We need to *see* something else to *be* something else.

Another path is to make a drastic change in your life. It might be time to fulfill a dream, accomplish a goal, or complete a project that has been on the back burner of an unfulfilled life. We know we want more. We don't exactly know what it is. We don't know how to get there. But we must claw our way toward finding whatever it is that gets us out of our bondage.

You might uncover parts of yourself as you unwrap the frayed, gummed bandages of your sticky emotional flytrap.

Consider the fact that if we are that far along with our awareness, at least we know that we don't know. Be happy! This is a much better, more realistic view than to *not* know that we don't know.

Now, that's a journey that you don't want to take. If you don't know that you're missing something, how can you begin to look for it? I've met too many people who do not know that they do not know.

We must learn about ourselves, and we must learn how to interact with others.

We must pray for enlightenment.

A powerful life experience can wake us up. We have to hope it happens to us.

Or we have to make something happen and hope that what we choose puts us on the road to awakening.

The good news is that you can expect a different life. You will be stronger, able to manage discord, confident enough to uphold your convictions. You will think highly enough of yourself to not gossip.

Most people have it wrong about gossip. We don't really think less of those we talk about. The scary truth is that we think less of ourselves. We have low self-esteem and a poor self-image when we try too hard to make someone else look bad.

To prove this theory has validity, ask yourself what you have to prove when you try to make someone else lose face. It's your own face you're losing. And what's the point of the point you want to make? The answer to these questions will help you understand what diminished emotional capacity can do to the quality of all your relationships.

If you choose to take the journey of self-discovery and you land safely on your own two feet, you can expect to feel a whole lot better. There are no guarantees, but you should find yourself more ready and open to accept a lot of what happens between and among the people you interact with. You might find that you are not as oppositional as you once were. You might find less of a need to interrupt or to finish someone else's sentence. You might be less judgmental.

One of the best things that might happen is that you will learn to be selective about to whom you choose to bare your soul. And even at that, if you're that brave, and you do not get the response you were hoping for, you will be able to walk away emotionally unscathed.

You might feel disappointed, but you probably won't feel anxious, hopeless, helpless, lost, agitated, afraid, and out of control.

Believe it or not, you will be at peace. You will finally have enough strength and faith in yourself to know you can breathe freely. This, readers, is true freedom. True personal freedom. True peace. The only kind.

- Take a long, hard look at yourself before you look at someone else. You'll always find something to work on.
- Listen twice as much as you talk. We have two ears and one mouth.
- Don't complain! You will become powerless.
- Eliminate negative thoughts, feelings and words from your daily communication.
- Get over your own importance.
- Brush the chip off your shoulder.
- Be grateful.
- Practice humility.

Twenty-Four

The Roads Not Taken

We missed a lot. There were no vacations and no new clothes, no new cars, new furniture, or home improvements. I always wished for a bedroom set. We lost out on some comfort, and unfortunately—more importantly—we lost too much precious time preparing for life.

Because of debilitating, life-altering, incurable illness, teenage marriage, abject poverty, and having no parents or mentors to guide them, my parents hit the ground running into a brick wall.

From day one, they were in true, authentic survival mode. Believe me, you have no time for extras when you are physically taking care of seven people without any resources to do so.

We needed people to rescue us from bleak hopelessness. We needed just a little individual attention, maybe a suggestion here and there, maybe a nod toward knowing what a family dinner or discussion looked like. But there was nothing but hardship. I'm sure I did not eat three meals a day, and if I didn't, I'm sure my parents and siblings didn't, either.

My mother moved like a robot, jumping from task to task, cooking, cleaning, washing clothes, drying them by hand, hanging sheets, grocery shopping, running errands, emptying the garbage, doing dishes, bathing us, and then getting ready for the next day.

I understand why there was no time for bedtime stories, conversations after school, play dates, sports, dance lessons, or trips to the library. How could we have fit that in?

Although my parents faced ongoing hardship and challenges, they had five children by the time they were in their early thirties. How do you feed a family of seven on a few thousand dollars a year? And after you pay rent and eat, how much money do you have left over to do much of anything else?

They spent their sixteen-hour days continually moving, mentally and physically, hurting from abandonment and suffering from loss. The depth of and damage from their emotional deficits was evident in our lack of awareness and social skills. None of us had a sense of self or knew how to interact with others.

This is what happens when you're put together with missing parts. And if and when you wake up, it's late in the game. You think you can make up for lost time, but the honest truth is, you cannot. The fact of the matter is, you're left with the time you're left with, and you have to make the most of it. You have to face the truth.

> *You cannot swim in the tangled wake of debris that surrounds your inadequate life.*

My parents could not go back in time to catch up. They met as teenagers, and they knew the passion of young, unadulterated love. They would never know the feeling of being in love, being rejected, and being able to move forward because they might not have been good for one another.

Every day of their lives together was filled with uncertainty, fear, insecurity, hardship, anxiety, anger, and contempt for the unknown invisible enemy of emotional bankruptcy.

They would never have the experience of planning a "normal" life together and having their dreams come true.

The normal events and scenarios (good and bad) in making a life together are supposed to happen, so that we grow and learn to manage positive *and* negative emotions. We are supposed to learn how to manage happiness and disappointment. We are humbled by the joy in our lives and at the same time, we can sit with our discomfort.

We move through it and survive, self-esteem intact, without becoming pathetic or apathetic, without making choices that wind up hurting us in the end. This growing process, in which we make mistakes and are able to recover, saves us from a lot of angst later on.

When you marry young or for the wrong reasons, changing your mind is much more complicated in the wake of divorce courts and alimony payments.

No, you cannot go back and relive your life. You cannot find what you have lost. You cannot put the pieces of the puzzle together so that it all fits together in a perfect little square. Mistakes are costly—sometimes too expensive to repair.

Pieces are missing. If you find them, you tuck them away and carry them in your heart. Hurtful as they are, they tug at you and remind you of the painful awakening and realization of how much you have to do in the third and final chapter of your life—or in whatever time you have left. It depends on your age of awakening.

Twenty-Five

WAKE UP BEFORE IT'S OVER

There are plenty of books that tell us how to reclaim our lives. Motivational speakers collect hefty fees for speeches that promise us a better life in ten easy steps. What they don't tell us is that we have lost a lot of time and there is absolutely no way to get it back. It's just that simple. We are kidding ourselves to think otherwise. Lost is lost.

We must be honest with ourselves. Without honesty, we cannot get better.

If you wake up at sixty, hopefully, you still have twenty good years of living in the moment. Maybe! The beginning of your life is when you have that defining moment. Start counting, adding, and subtracting. Don't fool yourself, because numbers don't lie.

Millions of people can live and die and never realize what they have missed. We might *feel* as if something is missing. We might even have some level of awareness to know that something is wrong. But for too many of us, we don't know what it is.

Also, there is plenty of advice on how to treat symptoms we are already aware of. This is the slippery slope. How do you get help for something you don't know you have? How do you make something right when you don't know what's wrong? How do you rein yourself in from being "out there?"

Something serendipitous could happen. Maybe, but don't count on it.

Think of your life in layers.

First:

Try to get in touch with aspects of your daily life. At first, think small. Focus on your daily routine and ask yourself if you're comfortable and happy with it.

Do you get enough sleep? Do you like where you sleep? Do you like your surroundings? Can you relax? How do you feel when you wake up in the morning? Is your bed comfortable? Do you look forward to going to sleep?

Do you eat well? Do you have access to good food? Do you know what that means?

Are you clean and organized? If not, how does that make you feel?

Next:

Do you have all the basic things necessary for survival? Do you feel peaceful? Are you satisfied with your station? Your profession, trade, or career?

Do you know that all work is honorable? Do you earn enough money to live, to be happy, if not necessarily to buy pleasure? There is a big difference, and you must know what it is.

Finally:

Do you have unfinished business—something you have always wanted to do and yet find a million excuses not to? Are you living your own life? Are you who you were meant to be? Are you fulfilled? Sustained? Centered? Confident?

Are there maybe one or two people with whom you can share any thought or to whom you can say out loud anything you feel without fear of loss and without qualification?

This is freedom in a relationship, and it is something that all people need and are looking for—whether they know it or not, whether they admit it or not. It is the most basic human need to be heard and to feel free to use our voices. Run fast from those who suppress that. Run away as fast as you can.

After you have completed your physical checklist, think about where you are in your emotional life. Think long and hard. Make a timeline of your life and see if you feel good about the events to date. Are certain decades better than others? Can you associate milestones with growth? What are they? Write them down.

Think about the people in your life. Are they emotionally deprived? Can you see yourself at least enough at this point to recognize that you are attracting people who are on the same emotional level that you are?

During the attraction phase, couples are drawn to each other because of good looks and other physical characteristics. We settle with each other on a level emotional playing field. When one partner grows more quickly, there are problems.

When one partner is being eaten alive by an emotional parasite, there are problems.

We feel comfortable with whatever our normality is. This is where we need to discover something outside of our own normality so we can realize there is another side to life. When we don't, we propagate in blind faith, in blind sight, in blind hope. We live our whole lives blind.

You might be in an abusive marriage. You might be a doormat for your friends. You might have typical outlets and ways of self-medicating to manage your frustration, lack of self-esteem, or loss of identity, like compulsive shopping, overspending, overeating, gambling, drinking, taking drugs, bullying, bossing others, shutting people down, building yourself up, gossiping or criticizing others—all of this when you have no clue that you need to spend time on improving yourself!

You might be an emotional parasite, feeding off others, bleeding others dry, making them sick—and yes, ultimately killing them.

You might be an emotional slave. You might have given yourself away for free—for nothing!

Twenty-Six

LIFE ISN'T FAIR

This is probably one of the most damaging thoughts we can have. Yes, life is not fair. That is an understatement.

We all know people who have had curveballs thrown at them. And we know there are survivors and casualties. Some can get through to the other side. Some remain stuck in the quagmire of emotional and mental gridlock. We have choices when life isn't fair. How do we make the right ones? What enables us to go through the decision-making process successfully?

For one thing, it takes a whole lot more than cognitive intelligence to be able to think critically and manage ourselves emotionally. We might be the smartest people in the world. We might even be successful at work. But surprisingly, if we have an emotional deficit, it can preclude us from being able to manage ourselves and our relationships. We need strength, and there are no fortifiers.

Without emotional stability and a crystal-clear view of ourselves and others, we will never become who we were meant to be.

Like my father, we are full of energy but running on empty. His deficit was more complicated and much more difficult because he had profound physical and emotional disabilities.

We had emotional disabilities and didn't know it. Can you imagine living like this? Yes, you can, if you examine your own life from this perspective. Unless you are rock solid and scrappy enough to catch every curveball with a golden glove, you know the pitfalls of navigating an uneven playing field.

You wish for peace and stability, but instead, you're in the fight of your life every day, dodging bullets that are riveting from all directions in your overloaded, confused brain and broken heart.

Seek and You Might Not Find. Keep Looking.

Emotional deficit yields a lot of insecurity and a big inferiority complex.

You have a vague idea of what you might need. But you have no idea about what you are entitled to. You don't know the feeling of wanting anything more than what you absolutely need to survive. Having breakfast, lunch, and dinner on the same day is a luxury. You have no control over such an important part of your life.

The fact is that because you don't know what is normal, you don't know how to ask for it. With a poor self-image, you lack the emotional strength to ask for anything.

You need confidence to ask. You need resilience to accept *no* for an answer.

You need stability and centeredness to know the direction you will take.

As a child, you feel like an orphan with a family. As an adult, you are part of a family of orphans. People are biologically related, but everyone is emotionally disconnected. Bonds cannot be broken because they were never formed.

Twenty-Seven

CASUALTIES IN THE WASTELAND

The most immediate protection we can hope for in the fight against emotional assailants is a level of awareness that we must acquire—no matter what it takes to do so. I'm not saying we should sell our souls to the devil to learn a hard lesson. I'm saying that if you feel emotionally violated in any way, you must get help. Otherwise you will lose years of living a healthier life.

How do we know when we are emotionally violated? Let's go back to the premise that a lot of us live in a fog because of a lack of awareness. Okay, now let's begin to be mindful of other aspects of our lives besides how we feel.

Why? Because our emotions manifest themselves in various behaviors when we are not whole.

Are you nervous? Hypervigilant? Sensitive to noise or touch? Do people's mannerisms and voices annoy you? Do you always feel unsettled? Is it difficult to relax? Do you sleep too much or not enough? Do you give or take too much? Not enough? Do you have a keen sense of injustice but feel you have no way to voice your opinion?

Are you bullied by a spouse, a child, a parent, a friend? Are you a bully?

Do you second-guess decisions you make? Can you make a decision? Do you compare yourself to others? Do you wish for what others have? Do you have any idea of how to get what you need? Do you expect to get more than you are willing to give? Do you give and never get anything in return?

Can you accept a compliment? Can you give one? Can you say you are sorry? Can you delay an impulse? Are you motivated? Do you always have to make your point? Do you have to be right? Are you critical of others?

Are you able to compromise? Do you talk only about yourself? Do you listen? Do you accuse people of things you are guilty of?

Do you ask questions? Can you give a straight answer? Are you afraid to answer?

Can you give an opinion? Can you accept an opinion you disagree with? Can you handle discord and disagreement? Do you talk in circles?

Do you have empathy? Do you need empathy? Do you know what you need? If so, can you ask for it?

Do you settle easily? Are you easily settled? Are you aggressive? Are you passive-aggressive? Do you get along with others?

Are your failed relationships always the other person's fault?

Do you know what balance and reciprocity are?

Do you expect others to do as you do—or to do as you say?

These are just some ways emotional illness shows itself in our everyday lives.

Our behavior often reflects our feelings. Unfortunately, we don't take the time to analyze every physical aspect of our lives. We are stuck in the emotional gridlock and are not aware enough of how we are acting—how we are actually living our lives.

Twenty-Eight

SEVEN DECADES OF REALIGNMENT

From my earliest days of living in abject poverty in my grandmother's crowded apartment in Brooklyn to living (seventy years later) in a retirement community comprising mostly middle-class senior citizens, my life has taken several twists and turns along the roads I traveled—often with too many pebbles in my shoes.

Today, I am grateful for everything I have and for everywhere I have been, although humbly I say that the cost of survival was, at times, a little more than I could afford. Often, I was surprised that I lived through episodes that I now see were terrifying.

This is what I mean by *frame of reference* and *self-awareness*. We know only what we know at any particular moment. We cannot know what we will know tomorrow. Normality is our own subjective, unique normality.

I had gripping, debilitating anxiety throughout most of my life. I groveled and grappled and apologized and qualified for almost fifty-five years. Then one day, while standing in my kitchen, I felt the currents of transformational electricity run through my veins. In that moment, I could see myself from a third-person perspective. I could look at myself—outside of myself.

It was a disturbing view. It was an awakening.

I was infused with energy I had never had before, the energy of awareness and mindfulness—a crystal-clear view of what I must do, and there was no turning back. No excuses. Most remarkably, there was no lack of emotional energy.

Because that's what was missing. Emotional energy. It took me fifty years to wake up and to be able to feel myself, to feel my own energy.

One scenario that might illustrate what lack of awareness feels like is to imagine talking to a group, maybe giving a speech, and being so nervous that we hear our own words but they do not feel as if they belong to us. Or we can be part of a conversation physically and afterward realize that we were not really present in the moment.

Blind Sight

The words are not part of our performance or behavior. We are detached from the interaction. We are not grounded, not emotionally present, not emotionally invested, not emotionally centered. We were not listening to ourselves and certainly not to others. We have no idea what was said. We heard, but we didn't listen.

We are there physically; the words are coming out of our mouths, but we are in a fog. Or we can pretend to listen, never really knowing what authentic, active listening is. The difference between hearing and listening is deafening.

We can live our entire lives in this way, detached from ourselves, attached only to a perceived reality. What is real? What is our perception? How are the two related? Which one is more important?

When we wake up, when we become mindful, patient, agreeable, softer, approachable, forgiving, slower to respond, not reactionary, with enough control not to react; when we listen, accept, reach out—only then can we say we are on track to being able to acquire the skills necessary to become whole. We can reach inside of ourselves and pull ourselves out of emotional bondage.

In this transformational moment, it dawned on me that I could go to college to earn a degree. I could get rid of this rope around my neck; it was choking me with insecurity and the strangling fear of being found out.

I was successful in my own business as a copywriter and advertising executive. I was earning a decent amount of money. But always, the voice in my head kept telling me I was not good enough, not complete enough, not successful enough, not whole—because I did not have an education.

Always, I could hear my parents' voices saying the words:

"You won't ever amount to anything without a college degree."

I always felt inferior, no matter how much I knew about anything. I never felt my opinion was justified. I did not feel confident about convictions and beliefs I held. If they were tested, I caved.

Because of emotional deprivation and low self-esteem, I was not good at detecting the perpetrators, the emotional assailants, those who keenly recognized vulnerability and confused kindness for weakness. Not only was I not able to see myself, I could not see anyone else, either.

I took people at face value and knew nothing about agenda setting. Never did it enter my mind that someone could show up at an event with a particular rehearsed script in mind, targeted at the pathetic prey.

Sometimes one partner steps on the other's toes too many times without apologizing for it. Your feet get sore, and your voice gets lost in the hustle and bustle of dancing around the issues.

Blind Sight

You hobble and wobble through your life, tottering around in the midst of drama on the stage that has become your life. You have nothing to hold on to.

You are going through the motions of living every day—but living without direction or focus or a plan of how to assemble the pieces of your broken self.

I desperately needed what postsecondary education would offer me. I am forever indebted to the professors whose teachings changed my life.

Likelihood and Probability

We are statistics.
You—the teenager
And me, the firstborn to an eighteen-year-old

We managed and made it
Through good times and bad
We turned out okay.
We prove that statistics lie.

You were never the type to coddle.
You were certainly not a blind mother—ha!
You didn't have time to read and sew.
But I picked up a few things along the way.

You told me to be generous and
To remember those who had less
All people are the same.
You told me to appreciate everything I had.
To not take anything for granted.

Take responsibility for myself.
Stand on my own two feet.
You never made excuses to protect me.

Twenty-Nine

STICK TO YOUR CONVICTIONS

I have spent a major portion of my life worrying about what other people thought and having anxiety if they didn't agree with me. I am enjoying the newfound freedom of letting go and embracing the courage of my convictions. Finally, I am comfortable with my opinions and feel entitled to own them. I can stand up for myself.

After all, an opinion is simply an opinion, and it belongs only to the person who holds it. A lot of people confuse opinion with fact, which causes a lot of unnecessary arguments and a tragic waste of precious time and emotional energy. I wish someone had told me.

For instance, there is no such fact as "best." There is no guaranteed best.

"Best" is simply someone's view. Yet we speak as though we have the final word on something like the "best" restaurant, the "best" cruise line, the "best" doctor.

It is so incredibly difficult to arrive at a verdict of "best." Why are people so hung up on something they can never prove? It is truly a matter of our values, beliefs, and *opinions*. We own them.

Opinions come from our own frame of reference and experience, and they are totally subjective. You can share an opinion. You can disagree. But you cannot force another person to agree with you, much in the same way that you cannot force someone to listen. I cannot tell you how much pain I caused myself and others simply by arguing over differences of opinion. Why do we care so much when someone does not agree with us? It seems crazy, right?

My parents spent most of their lives arguing horribly over differences of opinion, not statements of fact. Because of insecurity and instability and a lack of the confidence that could have enabled them to accept each other's views, they were children in adult bodies vying for recognition from each other—the validation they needed to become whole.

Because they lacked emotional strength and were never properly socialized, they did not have the courage of their own convictions to hold up during a simple disagreement or argument or against a different point of view.

This is just one example (of many) of how others affect you when you are not centered, when you do not have self- and social awareness, and when you lack self-confidence and self-identity. You are easily shaken.

You can tell a lot about someone when he or she doesn't agree with you. I am ashamed of my own behavior. Can I forgive myself because I didn't know any better? I don't know—but happily, I can tell you why it happened, what caused it, and maybe how to try to fix it.

Thirty

Tangled Up in Glue

It is like trying to untangle a cat's fur ball when you wake up to the realization that you've made mistakes you cannot fix and wasted time you cannot get back.

How do you start all over again?

It is a complicated process to unravel the cross strings of a life that is full of regret and bad decisions. But we set our own traps.

It is also complicated because the regret and poor decision-making come from feeling threatened, uncomfortable, insecure, afraid, small, inferior, and ill equipped to manage ourselves when we interact with others.

With so few resources, how can we cultivate a better sense of self that taps into who we really are or who we could be? How do we reach our destiny? What if we don't have the emotional strength to put ourselves out there, to trust others, to show vulnerability? What keeps us from getting the word out?

Malignant Self-Love

- I have twenty-twenty vision but have lived my whole life blind.
- I can see everything but myself.
- I preach that I am in a good place. The place where I reside is full of gossip, ill will, toxicity, vengeance, resentment, and guilt.
- I hear what you say. But I never listen.
- I expect to get much more than I am willing to give.
- I have expectations of things that are coming to me.
- I am confused about the difference between a good self-image and malignant self-love.
- I don't know what acknowledgment means.
- I use anecdotal information as a response mechanism.
- I am an interesting speaker. I speak often about myself.
- I am a sentence hijacker. I can finish your sentences, find the right word, and complete your last thought.
- I am paying attention only to what I am going to say next.
- I relate everything to myself.
- I take everything you say personally.
- I am a victim. I am victimized.
- I host weekly pity parties.
- I am bigger than life when I walk into a room.
- I expect everyone to move over for me.
- I have suffered more than anyone else.
- My life has been harder than anyone else's.
- I have had more challenges than anyone else.

- I have had to work for everything I have.
- I have received no lucky breaks as others have.
- I expect people to realize how much I have suffered.
- I don't care how much other people go through.
- I enjoy telling every microscopic detail of my life.
- I don't ask any questions.
- I expect people to listen intently.
- I am not interested in what you have to say.
- I wear an expression on my face that is repugnant.
- I am hypervigilant about my own thoughts when people are speaking.
- I complain about everything.
- I expect the world to revolve around me.

Thirty-One

FIRST STEPS IN THE THIRD DECADE

The year was 1960. It was a time when people were leaving New York City's five boroughs and migrating to New Jersey or Long Island for the promise of a better life in suburbia—a greener life with trees, flowers, and single-family homes.

My father worked for a company that was relocating to New Jersey, so we had to move. It wasn't as if my parents decided that it was time to leave the brick, concrete, iron, and steel three-bedroom apartment we rented from the New York City Public Housing Authority.

What would public high school in New Jersey be like after Catholic school in Brooklyn for eight years?

In addition to having strict parents who were not nurturing, I had nuns who slapped us across the face if they misread an expression or if our ill-fitting wool skullcaps fell off our heads.

Every few days in the month of May, in the fourth grade, we would crown the statue of the Blessed Mother with a fresh wreath of baby roses. The crown was about six inches in diameter. To this day, I can remember thinking I had never seen anything so beautiful. The size and color of the roses were amazing.

Maybe it was the first time I had ever seen fresh flowers. But even if it wasn't, these were special because they were perfectly arranged in a circle, so delicate and small.

I wanted to crown the statue so badly; I thought I would die if I didn't get chosen. But I was never one of the handful of girls to have the privilege of leading the procession of sixty fourth-graders around our crowded classroom to the front of the room where the porcelain Blessed Mother rigidly stood on top of a small table, draped with a white cloth and decorated with green twigs, which I now realize must have come from the florist who supplied the fresh crown of roses.

Crown of Roses with Thorns

It's the crown of roses that bothers me.
Someone chosen to place it on the marble head
Of the Holy Virgin Mother
Immaculate Mary

Chalk face, granite-pink shallow
Faintly sprinkled plaster of Paris
Chastity

Woman above all women
Mother of the Most High on earth
Explain to the nine-year-old
Picking favorites
Little freckled girls
Dirty from living in two rooms of ten
Whiteness like the statue
Religious icons
Soldiers marching
Filthy in principle
Worship thee above all others
Punish others who don't
Kiss your feet

Each day I was filled with anxiety and a breathless desire for my name to be called. But I never heard my own name. Instead, the same four girls were chosen over and over again during the entire merry month of May.

I mentioned to a couple of friends that I thought our teacher had favorites because she always picked the same four students to lead the procession and crown the porcelain Virgin Mother.

Somehow my teacher found out what I had said. One day, she asked me about it in front of the whole class. I owned up to my words.

Suddenly, she grabbed me by the hair and dragged me up to the front of the classroom, where she slapped me across my face repeatedly, from side to side.

Then, with one hand pulling my hair out of my head, she banged my head into the blackboard a few times with her other hand, screaming about the fact that I had said she played favorites. I was nine or ten years old.

So after all the hair pulling, yanking, banging, hitting, slapping, yelling, and screaming, as I stood there disheveled, degraded, debased, and demeaned, she ordered me to return to my desk, where I assumed the position of a good Catholic schoolgirl and continued with my work. My head hurt, and my hair was falling out.

When I got home from school, I told my mother what had happened. When my father got home from work, she told him what had happened. They both agreed they would not say anything about it to the monsignor, with whom they were close at the time. The school was part of our church, of which he was the head. So they let the whole thing go—completely. But I couldn't forget.

Throughout my life, I wanted to get in touch with my former teacher, the bully who went unpunished. Then, I wanted to get in touch with her children to tell them about their mother. I also mentioned the event a couple of times throughout my life to my mother, and she looked at me and said, "Really, is that how we responded? Oh, that's not too good."

Off Balance

She keeps you on edge
It's always about her.
You pay attention
Hypervigilant
It's never about you.

You're trained to anticipate the other's needs.
You ask all the questions.
All that matters is what's important to her.

She keeps taking.
You keep giving.

You don't have the right to dislike anything.
You have something wrong with you.
One-sided
No flip side.

You keep going back for more.
Fear of displeasing keeps you on guard.
Careful about how you say things
You're walking on raw eggs

She waits. You jump.

I learned a lot throughout my eight years of unrelenting fear and blind obedience at Catholic school with the nuns and priests. Amazingly, in a classroom that was overcrowded by today's standards, one nun was able to effectively teach sixty students. We were academically ready for high school at the end of eighth grade.

When I entered ninth grade, I was ahead of most of my public-school friends, who had never attended a parochial or private school. I knew vocabulary, geography, and arithmetic. I knew how to write a high-school essay. I knew English grammar. I acquired this knowledge and know-how from doing book reports and taking spelling tests. One teacher got through to sixty of us without aides or multiple classrooms.

Through all the corporal punishment and strict rules, we learned and were well prepared to enter high school. We were proud of where we came from. We went to *Catholic* school! It was an honor and a privilege.

By the time we moved to New Jersey, I was looking forward to going to a public high school where you wore regular clothes, like skirts and blouses, like you saw on *American Bandstand*—no more uniforms!

I would be able to wear something different every day. This was unfamiliar territory and an exciting part of becoming a teenage girl.

Blind Sight

My father took me shopping a few weeks before school started, and he bought me one blouse and two skirts. It was August. Both skirts were flannel with small pleats from the waist. Girls were not allowed to wear slacks, so we had a choice of only skirts or dresses. Some students wore kilts, which looked nice with knee socks and saddle shoes.

I got my first job at fifteen at a variety store, where I earned enough money to buy myself some clothes. However, I remember feeling pangs of envy when some of my friends had several expensive, beautiful Cos Cob blouses, gorgeous Shetland wool sweaters, and a variety of skirts and kilts that looked fabulous on them—not to mention their warm, boiled-wool Austrian Loden coats or stadium coats with leather toggle closures.

I yearned for some of these prized garments. I had just enough to get by. I looked okay, but believe me, I was on the other side of the best-dressed list.

These school experiences were lessons in what? Yes, our experiences only make us stronger. Ha, I love that statement: "They made us who we are today." Well, who exactly are we?

The truth is that a young person who is forced to be subservient to those in power has no voice in the discipline or decision-making process. In the 1950s and 60s, our teachers were devoted, committed adults who came to work every day, enthusiastic to teach and determined for us to learn.

We, in turn, always respected authority. We would never question a teacher, a coach, a guidance counselor, a principal, or an advisor. That's just the way it was.

Even though public school was not as strict as Catholic school, students definitely respected their teachers, and we knew our roles. It was unthinkable to answer back, to interrupt, to question, or to dispute an issue.

I think people in general were more obedient in the first seventy-five years or so of the twentieth century.

Thirty-Two

Emotional Deficits

I completely relinquished what little sense of myself I had when I got lost in finding and rescuing someone else. In balancing the challenge of being in a relationship at sixteen, I got gridlocked in codependence, confusion, and chaos. My ego (or, some would argue, the lack thereof) took over, and I was consumed with and driven by the lust of energetic teenage love.

> All the while, I'm looking for something
> I am not going to find.
> Looking in all the wrong places
> Thinking you'd be Mr. Fixit
> Waiting for answers that never came

> All the while, I'm hoping for something
> I cannot have
> Hoping in all the wrong people
> Expecting to find it in you
> Waiting for you to plant roots
> Instead cleaning up broken stems
> Dead seeds in the mix

I didn't know who I was, and looking back, I can see truth in the old adage that "youth is wasted on the young." Boy, did I waste time. But that's what you do when you have no sense of self, when you are disconnected, "out there," lost, breathing every day but not living. You are in a juvenile fog.

It's horrifying to realize the amount of time we waste living in a vacuum and thinking all the while that, like talented basketball players, we "see the floor."

It's a sad state of affairs, and it happens to so many of us. We are a pathetic lot, groveling because of undeserved low self-esteem.

This disconnect is the result of being emotionally impoverished—feeling acute emotional deprivation on all levels. Money is only a small part of the deficit.

How can we be present in the moment? What will enable us to see clearly and accurately into who we are at various stages of our lives?

Blind Sight

Think about your favorite book or movie. You had an opinion about it. You got a feeling; you connected with what you read or what you saw.

Now go back and read that same book or watch that same movie, as long as it's been at least ten years. I'm going to say you'll come away with a different view.

The book and movie have not changed, but you have.

This is one way of explaining how we can see life only through our own eyes and our own frame of reference, according to where we are at that time in our lives. Our knowledge and experience are the interpreters of the words and images. Our view changes as we grow, and so does the meaning of everything around us.

If we don't grow, if we are cursed with arrested development, things remain the same, and that's when we get stuck. Our stunted growth places us into a dreaded gridlock that paralyzes us, blinds us, and, pitifully, keeps us from becoming who we were meant to be.

This is one of the worst things that can happen to anyone. And it's frightening that we can live our entire lives and never realize this has happened. We can walk along the path of life in some kind of narcoleptic sleep.

So how do we wake up? What is it that makes us see ourselves and other people as clearly as possible? Something daunting and powerful…something unplanned and uninvited. Or a plan whose outcome may not be exactly what we had in mind. When this happens, we are surprised by the outcome, grateful for the transformation, and accepting of our newer selves. We are awestruck by our new invention or reinvention of ourselves.

Ah, we are on our way to enlightenment. We become anxious to get going. We want to begin living life, seeing the same things in a different way, seeing ourselves, forgiving ourselves for being shortsighted but knowing it wasn't possible to take the journey along a different road at a different time. Ah——but we got there! Not so fast.

Blind Sight

Distorted Views

Inside out
Outside in
Clear view
Fogging up the mirror

I see you through the glass
Clear etchings of your faults
Blank slate of myself
Critical pictures of others
Missing pieces of myself
Missing clues

There is no way to tell
The impact of hell
On the living
You think you might know
You pray it won't show

To-Do List

- You cannot create chaos by yourself.
- Be provisional. People will be drawn to you.
- Know that you don't know.
- Judge character by how someone handles power.
- People know when you are kidding yourself.
- Find your blind spot.
- Be true to yourself in the words that you say.
- Say what you mean and mean what you say.
- The higher you climb, the lower the platform.
- You need to run into yourself.
- Trust your intuition. It's the sum of your knowledge and experience.
- Live from the inside out.
- Be your authentic self.
- Guard your vulnerability.
- Attention is your most precious commodity. Give it sparingly.
- Understand and be understood in the purest sense.
- Ask questions—but never of people who don't listen.
- Behave so as to eliminate control.

Thirty-Three

Brooklyn, 1950s

There was more that happened in the projects in Brooklyn. I witnessed a home invasion at nine years old as I stood in the long, narrow, tiled, concrete hallway, knocking on my friend's cold, painted-steel front door, waiting for her to come out of her apartment. A wooden door? Ha! I had never seen one.

On another day, in the courtyard of the tenement buildings, I was repeatedly punched in the face, chest, and stomach by a friend as his mother held my hands behind my back.

And the worst of what happened is when I was attacked by two men in the hallway of our apartment building. I was six. I remember it was right after dinner, and I was on my way to my friend's apartment. Suddenly, I was on my back, and I felt hands on my knees, when all of a sudden the outside door burst open, and in walked two neighbors who broke up the assault. Their timing was perfect.

They saved me. The memory is vivid. I was lying on a cement floor in front of an incinerator.

The men ran away. The neighbors helped me up and brought me home, which was about one hundred feet from the crime scene. They explained to my parents what had happened. When they left, my mother placed me in a large cardboard box and dragged me over to where my father was sitting so he could hit me with his belt and reprimand me for what had happened. He held me by my ankles and repeatedly slapped my bare behind. Yes, this, too, was my fault.

Blind Sight

Null and void
Are ideas I toyed
With

Barely alive

You
Glorified
Simplified
Two by two
Without shoes

Cannot walk
Just talk

Crucified!

On another day, on the rare occasion that I was with my mother, I remember sitting at our neighbor's kitchen table and learning that a fifteen-month-old baby boy had fallen to his death from our ten-story brick high-rise.

Looking back, I wonder: how did a child that age open the steel door to the stairway that led to each of the ten floors, go all the way up to the roof, walk to the edge, and fall or jump off? This just seems impossible.

Believe it or not, the story ends there. I remember some commotion over the horrific incident, some screaming, but that's about it.

A fifteen-month-old baby boy fell to his death by climbing (by himself?) to the roof of a brick building in the projects in Brooklyn. Yes, this really happened.

Thirty-Four

Recovering from Heart Dis-ease

You're in the fight of your life when your heart is on the mend. Someone has disconnected your blood supply for a while and put you on life support. You stay there until the arteries are cleared of debris and blood can once again flow unobstructed—so that you can live on your own.

Look out, everyone. You're moving with the fragile force of a roller coaster. Up and down, down and up, holding on through twists and turns. You hear rumbling noises inside and out. You'd better get all you can out of the ride and brace yourself—be ready for the abrupt halt! The door opens, and out you go.

During the ride, the fear and enthrallment of force erase everything else, unless you are in the minority of people who are not affected at all by outside forces.

Yes, there are some people like that. They survive, untouched, unscathed, no matter what. But as I said, they are the minority. The majority of us grip the handles in anticipation of just making it through, not fully aware of everything else that's going on around us. We have to hold on with everything we have in order to survive. And if we fall, there's no one else to save us, just like when we are on the roller coaster. The cyclone takes our breath away, and we become dependents—emotional codependents feeding off others' insatiable needs. Feeding the hungry and dying from emotional starvation.

"Ma, are you there?"

Epilogue

Family, friends, and advisors who have read this manuscript commented that some of the material was not as clear as it could be. I embraced this helpful insight and cut into the words where I thought they needed to be fleshed out.

My parents suffered morbidly from emotional malnutrition. Everything that happened to them soon after they got married as teenagers was just too much for them to manage by themselves—mostly because they were emotionally starved as children. Because of unforeseen and unfortunate circumstances—like illness and death—in the lives of their own parents, they were orphaned physically and emotionally. Can you believe they never realized what had happened to them?

Unequivocally, they had no support: no parents, no mentors, no older siblings, no extended family who could help, no nothing! It's true. It's miraculous that my father graduated from college and went on to become a writer and senior editor for major publishing companies. My mother went back to school at forty-five, in the middle of a physically daunting life, to become a nurse. They were remarkable, indeed, and determined to *never* give up. And they didn't!

I am so extremely proud to say they were my parents. Few people I know have accomplished so much without any resources. How they overcame poverty, major illness, homelessness, and lack of education and parental guidance is nothing short of a miracle. In the truest sense of the words, as precisely as I can articulate them, they did it *by themselves* without any help.

They did it, yes, but always weighed down by the heavy burden of emotional baggage and a level of frustration I cannot imagine. We always do better with options and choices. But I cannot think of a time when they had too many of them, at least when any options or choices they thought about would have been easily attainable.

The best place to be in life is to be at peace. No matter what we have in terms of tangible things we can hold in our hands, we will never feel whole if we are not emotionally healthy.

So even when my parents crawled their way out of hopelessness and began to scrape up and piece together the fragments of their broken lives, they forgot to first get in touch with what had happened to them. Because they never knew what they had lost, they couldn't begin to search for what was missing.

They fought and fought continually, each one telling the other what was wrong with him or her, never looking inward at themselves or wondering what role each of them played in their horribly dysfunctional relationship.

Also, because of their early parental abandonment and lack of emotional nourishment, they didn't know how to trust. Because they couldn't trust, they could never make themselves vulnerable. Neither of them knew how to ask for what he or she needed. Neither of them knew how to be emotionally involved. They were either in escape mode or in survival mode, and it never occurred to them that there was another way to live—in which people reach out to one another, rely on one another, and support one another in a safe, loving, reciprocal manner.

And because dysfunction breeds negative emotions like disgust, contempt, disappointment, sadness and fear, they became weaker and weaker emotionally until their nerves were ulcerated and raw. One wrong word or mistaken expression, and all hell broke loose. The eruptive, explosive, turbocharged storms were cries for help with frozen tears—the culmination of decades of longing for parental affirmation and attachment. They knew no such things.

And so their search for connection began when they met each other, but the chance to connect never presented itself because tragedy always got in the way.

As they say, "It's not what happens to us; it's how we handle it." Well, we need tools to handle "it."

Some people can handle things better than others; yes, they can— but not without being emotionally strong, emotionally nourished, emotionally balanced, and emotionally stable enough to handle curveballs and bumps in the road that come our way. We can't get rid of those pebbles in our shoes.

Sometimes, the deprivation is generational, passed on from one to the other, because you can't give what you don't have. I believe in my heart it's not done on purpose. I am not speaking about those people who hurt others on purpose—manipulators, emotional predators, people with agendas who inflict pain. They are not my audience. I have no knowledge of or experience in figuring out why someone could or would act that way, except to say it could be mental—not purely emotional, as I believe it was with my parents, my family, and me.

This is why it is critically important to realize your own emotional state and to begin the journey of getting what you need to become emotionally nourished. Emotional gridlock is not something that jumps out at us and is often not easily identified. All I know is that it can cause a lot of unnecessary grief if it goes unchecked. Try as hard as you can to get in touch with your own feelings. Dig deep!

My purpose is to reach out to those who might recognize in my story pieces of themselves—glimpses into or broad views of their lives. Some of us know what it's like to feel shame, blame, embarrassment, insecurity, hesitancy, uncertainty, apprehension, discouragement, and fear.

I felt all of these. But—when I established and enforced boundaries, embraced healthy communication, and broke the cycle of morbid codependency, a floodgate of self-discovery opened. The experience has been life changing.

I've never been jealous or envious of anyone, thank goodness. But I have been in too many situations (in my earlier life, my other life) in which I was surrounded by confident, emotionally strong people, and I remember being in awe, being impressed, but mostly being disappointed in myself.

I could do that! I thought. But no, I couldn't—not at the time.

But, believe it or not, after some hard work, it's entirely possible to nourish yourself to the point that the insecurity goes away. Yes, it really does! It dissolves; it dissipates into thin air.

You actually do *change*. You are the caterpillar—creeping along in the muck and mire—who becomes the butterfly, flying high and away, with sensors that are attuned to yourself and your own capabilities and to the environment around you. A metamorphosis has occurred!

My intention is not to make you feel worse than you already might feel. My intention is to help you by telling you that if you find yourself, if you find your place, your station, your purpose—if you fulfill your purpose—you can feel whole. That might help push the blinders off.

But you must become aware of yourself. Get in touch with your level of awareness—of yourself and of others. It's a lot of work but well worth the effort.

Grow and cultivate the garden of your life. Weed out roots that overpower new growth. Slowly throw away dead seeds in the mix.

You must do things that help you feel better about yourself. Achieve something, no matter how big or small! Yes, sometimes it's hard for us to know exactly what we can achieve because that's different for everyone.

Do something you love. Learn something new or something you want to know more about. Cultivate an interest in which you invest time and reap a reward. Get results that boost your self-confidence—feedback that makes you smile and jump for joy. You must learn how to feel good about yourself.

Go through the process of beginning and completing a project. Get in touch with how you feel with each task you finish. Be introspective about the positives and negatives of each experience. Examine all the variables involved in each project. Consider the most important aspects that contributed to your success. Ask yourself if you feel stronger after each small victory.

Earn a degree or a certificate; take a course; start a business; write and sell your poetry; play an instrument; organize your home; learn to cook; volunteer at the library, a hospital, or a soup kitchen. *Be kind!*

Kindness is an attribute that will help get you to where you need to be, and it will build self-esteem, self-worth, and self-identity. A kind person is a strong person.

Kindness is connected to emotional competency and maturity.

Surround yourself with upbeat people, not those who drag you down. Complainers and gossipers will drain you. Learn how to be a better friend and listen to a friend (but not to someone who doesn't listen to you). Remember, you cannot give your energy away, and you cannot stay in a one-way, one-sided, unbalanced relationship with *anyone*.

We are not here to fix people—no matter how much we think we know. And the truth is, we cannot fix anyone; it's hard enough to improve ourselves. Be wary of anyone who focuses his or her energy on trying to change you. Are you in a relationship with someone who wants to fix you?

Finally, overall, just learn how to take the best care of yourself that you possibly can. I'm not going to tell you to eat well, maintain a healthy weight, exercise, stretch every morning, keep a journal, meditate, and do yoga. You've heard all that before.

Here's the best part of becoming emotionally whole: the better we feel about ourselves emotionally, and the better fed we become, the more effortless it will become to implement the ubiquitous laundry list of self-improvement techniques. They are things we have already heard, things we already know but find impossible to embrace.

Open your eyes, ears, heart, hands, and mind! Read. Listen. Listen. Listen. Try speaking to a professional, but find someone who is trained in heart healing. Look hard at yourself before criticizing something you don't like about others; make sure you don't see the same quality in yourself.

Also, surround yourself with people who are interested in you. Stay in relationships that are interactive and reciprocal. You should feel free to express yourself (within boundaries). You should feel better—not worse—after you speak with someone. People should feel better—not worse—after speaking with you. A relationship is a two-way street. You cannot receive nourishment, and you cannot give it, if your relationships are not balanced. You're wasting your energy.

Look for kindness. Goodness. Gentleness. Generosity of spirit. Encouragement. Avoid aggression, hostility, contempt.

And if you are the one who is always talking about herself, never asking questions, never listening, never affirming or acknowledging what someone says to you…don't expect too much richness in your monochromatic, monopolistic monologue. Wake up and stop wondering why you have conflict in your life!

If you are critical of others, you must crash into yourself on that one-way street. If you think you are in a position to comment on another person's life, you're kidding yourself. You are not in a good place. No *ifs*, *and*s, or *but*s. You are not at peace. And yes, those with some awareness, those who are emotionally whole, can easily see where you are. Get help. Get honest. Get real.

Don't ever expect to get more than you're willing to give.

Run away as fast as you can if someone doesn't ask you questions…doesn't acknowledge what you say…responds with something about himself or herself…criticizes your thoughts…mocks your lack of knowledge on a particular topic…gets too annoyed if you don't agree with him or her…or tells you what you need to do…what you should do…to feel better. This, my friend, is not a friend!

Run. Run. Run. And don't look back.

You are no longer someone's little boy or girl. You are not under anyone's thumb. You are not subservient. Be cordial. Be nice. But save your emotional energy. Nourish yourself first. You will need sustenance for your journey and to give to others who are most worthy.

On the other hand, don't feel sorry for yourself. Don't look at what others have. They are not luckier or better off than you are. No one handed life to them on a platter of all good things piled high.

I contend they were emotionally whole earlier on. Someone nourished their souls, hearts, and minds. And I guess we could point to the rich and say they are luckier than some of us poorer souls. But if they are not emotionally whole, they, too, will make a mess of things because they are not surefooted on the path.

Money can buy pleasure, but it surely cannot buy happiness. We all know people who are well off financially and "bad off" in other areas of their lives.

If you feel uneasy, uncomfortable, unsure, unsettled, unsafe, unable…your feelings could be rooted in seeds that weren't properly planted and nourished, and so you didn't bloom on time.

There's hope and help. Uncover the truth. Pull yourself out from under the heap of junk that's been weighing heavily on your heart. You might not be suffering from a mental illness.

You might have an emotional disease. Dis-ease. Dis——ease. Dis…ease.

Ease-y is the place to be. You'll know it when you feel it.

Bibliography

Goleman, Daniel. *Emotional Intelligence: Why It Can Matter More Than IQ.* New York: Random House Publishing Group, 1995.

Wilson, Daniel J. *Living with Polio: The Epidemic and Its Survivors.* Chicago: Chicago University Press, 2005.

About the Author

Adeline Moore hails from Brooklyn, New York. In her work as a copywriter and advertising executive, she has written magazine articles, ad copy, website content, and marketing materials for some of the biggest companies in the world.

Moore received her master's degree in communication and information. She now works as an adjunct professor.

Made in United States
North Haven, CT
29 June 2024

54217697R00093